The Employer Brand

The Employer Brand®

Bringing the Best of Brand Management to People at Work

Simon Barrow and Richard Mosley

Simon Barrow

Richard Mosley

April 2007

John Wiley & Sons, Ltd

Copyright © 2005   John Wiley & Sons Ltd, The Atrium, Southern Gate, Chichester,
West Sussex PO19 8SQ, England

        Telephone (+44) 1243 779777

Email (for orders and customer service enquiries): cs-books@wiley.co.uk
Visit our Home Page on www.wiley.com

Reprinted March 2006

Other Wiley Editorial Offices

John Wiley & Sons Inc., 111 River Street, Hoboken, NJ 07030, USA

Jossey-Bass, 989 Market Street, San Francisco, CA 94103-1741, USA

Wiley-VCH Verlag GmbH, Boschstr. 12, D-69469 Weinheim, Germany

John Wiley & Sons Australia Ltd, 42 McDougall Street, Milton, Queensland 4064, Australia

John Wiley & Sons (Asia) Pte Ltd, 2 Clementi Loop #02-01, Jin Xing Distripark, Singapore 129809

John Wiley & Sons Canada Ltd, 22 Worcester Road, Etobicoke, Ontario, Canada M9W 1L1

Wiley also publishes its books in a variety of electronic formats. Some content that appears in print may
not be available in electronic books.

Library of Congress Cataloging-in-Publication Data

Barrow, Simon.
 The employer brand : bringing the best of brand management to people at work / Simon Barrow and
Richard Mosley.
  p. cm.
 Includes bibliographical references and index.
 ISBN 13 978-0-470-01273-4 (cloth : alk. paper)
 ISBN 10 0-470-01273-0 (cloth : alk. paper)
 1. Product management. I. Mosley, Richard. II. Title.
 HF5415.15.B375 2006
 658.3′14–dc22   2005020003

British Library Cataloguing in Publication Data

A catalogue record for this book is available from the British Library

ISBN 13 978-0-470-01273-4 (HB)
ISBN 10 0-470-01273-0 (HB)

Typeset in 12/14 Garamond by SNP Best-set Typesetter Ltd., Hong Kong
Printed and bound in Great Britain by TJ International Ltd, Padstow, Cornwall, UK
This book is printed on acid-free paper responsibly manufactured from sustainable forestry
in which at least two trees are planted for each one used for paper production.

To Sheena Barrow and Fiona Mosley

Contents

List of Illustrations

Acknowledgements

Many people have played a part in shaping the thinking in this book, but it would have been impossible without the thought-inspiring contributions made by the following people.

Greg Dyke, previous Director General, and Russell Grossman of the BBC; Alain Wertheimer of Chanel; Tracy Robbins and Tim Small of Compass Group; Ian Edgeworth of Greggs; Robert Hiscox and Bronek Masojada of Hiscox; Dr Stephen Harding and Nick Tatchell of ISR; Ken Temple of the John Lewis Partnership; Michael Robinson of Man Investments; Claire Henry of Microsoft; Tom Harvey of Nationwide Building Society; David Roberts of Orange; Camille Burrows of PepsiCo; Anne Marie Bell, Ivan Newman and John Reid-Dodick of Reuters; David Fairhurst of Tesco; Nigel Brocklehurst and Darren Briggs of Vodafone; Fergus Balfour, Rhodora Palomar Fresnedi, Yuko Miyata and Stephane le Camus of Unilever; and Sir Martin Sorrell of WPP.

Many of the above have kindly allowed us to put their portraits on the cover, in addition to the following colleagues, clients, alumni, advisors, consultants and friends of People in Business.

John Ainley, Geoff Armstrong, Becky Barrow, Trevor Beattie, Susana Berlevy, Kashmir Bilgan, Sir Christopher Bland, Richard Boggis-Rolfe, Omberline de Boissieu, Sir Thomas Boyd-Carpenter, Stephen Bubb, Doug Bugie, Christopher Carson, Tim Cole, Chris Darke, Colette Dorward, Rob Drewett, Jesper Edelmann, David Evans, Liam Fitzpatrick, Carmel Flatley, Keith Faulkner, Sir Malcolm Field, Fiona Fong, Richard Foster, Jane Francis, Rod Eddington, Julie George, Joanne Gilbert, Alison Grainger, Mike Haffenden, Colin Harris, Tom Harvey, Richard Haythorthwaite, Steve Holliday, Glyn House, Simon Howard, Hugh Jaques, Daniel Kasmir, Andrew Ketteringham, Brian Kingham, Andrew Lambert, Simon Lockett, Philip Marsden, Luke Mayhew, Jim McAuslan,

Tim Melville-Ross, Trevor Merriden, Richard Needham, Stuart Newton, Linda Nielson, David Norman, Nia Parry, Harvey Pearson, Amy Pike, Fabiola Pizzigalo, Amin Rajan, Alison Rankin-Frost, Sir Robert Worceste, Nikki Rolfe, Lynn Shepherd, Antony Snow, Andy Street, John Taylor, David Verey, Jonny Wates, Lady Bridgett Walters, Laura Whyte and Paul Williams.

We would also like to thank Compass Group for allowing us to feature a number of the portraits of high performing employees featured in their recent global employer brand campaign.

Preface

Books like this tend to get written for two main reasons. One is when the approach is new and the creators believe they have a missionary role to introduce a new point of view that will change the way everyone thinks. The second is when the area is well established but the writer wants to add a new dimension to a subject. This book combines aspects of both. For many this will be the first time they have come across this way of thinking. For others, the concept will be familiar, but its scope of application will be uncertain. Whichever camp you inhabit, we hope that this first book on the employer brand leaves you clear about its meaning and motivated to put the thinking into practice.

Given that I spent years in the advertising business before my work in human resources, here is a story about two books that have acted as models for this one. The first is Rosser Reeves' classic *Reality in Advertising*, a book that changed the way in which advertising is assessed and measured.[1]* Years ago at the Players Club in New York I met Charles Roman the copywriter who created Charles Atlas who gave hope to '97-lb weaklings who had sand kicked in their faces' on the basis that 'you too can have a body like mine'. Roman showed me a battered copy of Reeves' book in which the master had written: 'to Charles Roman who has been practising reality in advertising all of his life.'

David Ogilvy, the founder of Ogilvy and Mather, wrote a different kind of book about the same subject but it was more a celebration of what he thought was great about the business when it is done well. It was called *Confessions of an Advertising Man* and, with wit and grace, described his experiences and the philosophy that had built his agency.[2] It contained gems like 'the consumer isn't a moron she is your wife', 'salesmen

---

* Superscript figures relate to the References section at the end of the book.

don't sing', and the power of long copy, 'the more you tell the more you sell' accompanied by a brilliant description of the benefits of the Aga cooker written when he was a salesman for this new product in the 1930s.

Where does this book on the Employer Brand fit into such a format? The employer brand concept has already achieved substantial awareness among the HR community worldwide. In 2003 an employer brand survey conducted by *The Economist* among a global panel of readers revealed a 61% level of awareness among HR professionals and 41% among non-HR professionals.[3] Total awareness in the UK was 36%, with the highest awareness levels recorded in the USA (42%) and Asia-Pacific (45%). Of the 138 leading companies surveyed by the Conference Board in 2001, 40% claimed to be actively engaged in some form of employer branding.[4] Conference companies have been running events featuring the employer brand since 1996. I wrote this on the way back from running the first employer brand workshop in China and in recent years have spoken in most major markets.

SO WHY NOW?

The number one reason is that this approach lacks the definition and established rigour it needs. 'Employer branding' is too often limited to the look and feel of recruitment advertising or internal communication campaigns to sell the benefits of the employer as 'a great place to work'. These perspectives lack the depth that any recognition of the reality of the employment experience must have if it is to carry weight with employees actual or potential. Here is the definition that Tim Ambler of the London Business School and I wrote in 1996:

> We define the Employer Brand as the package of functional, economic and psychological benefits provided by employment and identified with the employing company.
> The main role of the employer brand is to provide a coherent framework for management to simplify and focus priorities, increase productivity and improve recruitment, retention and commitment.[5]

Secondly, we believe that, like good marketing, this is a fundamental approach to the way people are managed, listened to and involved. It isn't a fad. It is a way of working that will last indefinitely. Procter & Gamble created the brand management concept in 1931 and it has remained the basis for running effective customer-facing businesses ever since.

Thirdly, we believe that the Human Resource community needs this approach to provide the clarity, the focus and the internal platform that they need to pull together the plethora of activities that make up their responsibilities. We have seen the emerging strength of HR people when they have grasped the concept of employer brand management and it has provided them with the coherence and the zeal that marketing people have long demonstrated. This book is primarily for them and we hope that it will provide a touchstone and perhaps some inspiration. The employer brand approach is a powerful one but only when the sponsors are powerful and HR must be able to match the pitch of this ball. If they do not, then others will step into the vacuum. We are starting to see this happen with titles like 'Talent Manager', 'Resourcing Manager' and other initiatives from Organisational Development, Internal Communications and Marketing.

However, the message of this book is also needed by senior management. We will argue that the employer brand, and their personal commitment to it, can make a valuable contribution to overall corporate success. When management was about the command and control of hourly paid muscle workers in an environment that favoured capital rather than labour, then perhaps these thoughts were less relevant but those days ended years ago.

Returning to the themes with which I started this preface, this book has two authors, and in some respects represents two books in one. I will describe the origination of the Employer Brand concept and the circumstances that are demanding its acceptance by senior management. My colleague, Richard Mosley, will describe some of the practical steps involved in applying employer brand thinking to your organisation. We hope that this combination of context, motivation, and 'how to' will prove an effective formula.

This book could not have been written without the experience we have gained from the clients of People in Business, in particular Hiscox, Premier Oil, Unilever, Manpower, John Lewis, The Crown Prosecution Service and Man Investments, among others. We also want to thank those who have given us their time, including Tesco, Sainsbury's, Reuters, Microsoft, the BBC, Compass Group, Nationwide Building Society,

Orange, Vodafone and Sir Martin Sorrell, CEO of WPP, who is responsible for managing one of the most complex employer brands on earth.

Richard and I hope that this book will be useful, inspiring and relevant and that it will provide a helpful basis for all those who are endeavouring to make the employment experience in their organisations both attractive and mutually profitable.

Simon Barrow
March 2005

Part I

The Rationale for Change

Simon Barrow

Birth of an Idea 1

When I first thought of the idea of the Employer Brand it struck me as utterly obvious. There I was in a new HR-facing job and searching for the templates that had helped me to be a consumer goods brand manager and then CEO of an advertising agency in London. Good ideas often strike their creators as obvious probably because there is an urgent need to go about doing something in a better way.

In this case it was my arrival as CEO of a personnel business. In those days it was known as Charles Barker Human Resources, and it was part of the same group as the advertising agency I'd been running, which had recently been sold to our US partners NWAyer. I found myself in charge of an efficient factory producing 100,000 job ads a year, working for over 2000 clients and producing 5 million copies of house newspapers, dozens of graduate recruitment brochures and internal communications artefacts. Demand was driven by HR people within client organisations who themselves were under pressure from line managers seeking to fill jobs fast. Where, I wondered, was the agency planning and the research necessary to create a strategy that could pull together the organisation's efforts and guide not only the creative work but also the overall approach to the employment experience? If this was a consumer brand you wouldn't run it this way, but of course it isn't one, it's something else: it's an Employer Brand. That was the moment I saw things differently and have been trying to apply this perspective ever since in the 18 years that I have been involved in helping organisations to succeed by bringing out the best in their people.

I was lucky to have had the consumer goods experience that Colgate–Palmolive and Best Foods (now part of Unilever) had given me. The Prime Minister Harold Macmillan once said that it helped just once in a life to be associated with something that was absolutely first class, and that's how I felt about the eight years I spent in brand management. I was given responsibility and influence, though not power, on everything that was likely to have an effect on the health and strength of a brand. This included being expected to know the facts and have an opinion on the formula, packaging, identity, distribution, pricing, promotion, costs, margin improvement, advertising creative work, media selection, consumer and trade research. I was also expected to have the same information for each competitive brand. Brand management was created by Procter & Gamble in 1931 and has been taken up as a fundamental discipline ever since. It seemed reasonable to see what could be done to apply this thinking to the employer brand experience.

One of the factors that attracted me to Colgate as an employer was the location. Back in the 1970s it was just about the only top-ranking consumer goods business still based in Central London. Most were elsewhere: General Foods to Banbury, Mars to Slough and P&G to Newcastle. When I arrived there I found a remarkable group of fellow brand managers who found London life good for them both corporately and personally. They have all achieved something special since – Barrie Spelling, David Enfield, Tim Chappell, John Plackett, Patrick Bowden, and Martin Forde among others. I have sometimes wondered if the company ever considered the location aspect and whether the culture has changed markedly since moving to Guildford. They also paid better. When I moved there from Best Foods my basic salary rose 40%. There was no apparent career planning and I don't recall contact with anyone with an HR title. You were expected to make your own luck and, if you were any good, were to be ready and able to move to another Colgate location anywhere. That happened to me when I was 33 with an offer to move to Benelux as Marketing Director. The offer was made on a Thursday with a decision expected the following Monday. It was time to find a more independent life and after a few months I moved to the embryo consumer advertising business of the Charles Barker Group.

In terms of Employer Brand thinking, Colgate gave me the theory and practice in managing all the elements that make up a brand. Charles Barker provided the people management aspects, which ultimately are the key success factors, as Charles Barker was later to find out to their cost. After four years as an account director I became Managing Director and later Chief Executive of the consumer advertising business under the Ayer Barker name, reflecting a partnership with the long-established US agency NWAyer in New York. Ayer were famous for creating ads like 'Diamonds are forever' for De Beers, 'Reach out and touch somebody' for AT&T and the highly influential employer brand campaign for the US Army 'Be all that you can be'.

While people think that running an agency is solely about creativity and salesmanship, the reality is that your ultimate success is determined by recruiting, engaging and retaining good people. When Anita Roddick said, in her moving biography *Body and Soul*, 'My people are my first line of customers', that was entirely what I felt.[1] The great value of winning Sharp Electronics, Chanel, Mercedes-Benz, Barclaycard and Save the Children Fund among others was not just the income and the opportunity it provided to demonstrate our creative skills but the fact that it made the agency easier to sell to good people. The argument for joining was that this was an agency on the move. It wasn't staked out and therefore had plenty of opportunity and yet it had the backing of what was then the most prosperous communications group in the UK whose Chairman, Kyrle Simond, was by far the best paid boss of any agency group.

Some remarkable people came on board: Charles Channon as Head of Planning from J. Walter Thompson, Keith Ravenscroft from Ogilvy & Mather as a copywriter, shortly to be followed by Salman Rushdie who stayed five years and could be relied upon to understand the strategy and produce saleable if not brilliant work. When *Midnight's Children*[2] was accepted by Jonathon Cape, Salman told me that he wanted to leave the ad business. It was 1981 and we had been paying him £15,000 for a three-day week. Cape had told him that the minimum he could expect from the book in the first year was £22,000 and he felt confident enough to quit the business. When the book came out he sent me a copy with the somewhat double-edged inscription 'to Simon, who helped me write *Midnight's Children* three days a week'.

Looking back on those years in the consumer advertising business, there was one client for whom every step was the enhancement of the employment experience. That client was Avon for whom we were working, thanks to NWAyer in the US. I recall the UK MD Alan Daniels saying that the real purpose of the apparently customer-facing advertising 'Avon you make me smile' campaign of the time, was to get 40,000 representatives out of their homes and round to their neighbours selling Avon's products. They did not call it the Employer Brand back in the 1980s but Avon remain past masters in understanding and enthusing thousands of people round the world to spend time with their friends looking at what Avon have to offer.

After 10 years of running the agency it was time for a change. The Charles Barker Group was starting to build its already substantial HR stance and as part of the flotation had bought the executive recruiter Norman Broadbent, then approaching the height of its powers. My job as CEO was to develop Barker's HR business. If the Employer Brand concept was going to be taken seriously it had to impact senior management. I started to see the Human Resource Directors and, if possible, the CEO/MDs of the most significant clients. I would establish what they had spent with us in the last year and then explain that, in the UK in general, they were spending perhaps over £1m across numerous sites and from different budgets. Given that kind of money did they not deserve better research, and better coordination and discipline? It got us noticed and it established bridgeheads with senior clients through which the head of any agency can help, in the words of Martin Boase, founder of BMP, 'to prevent unfairness'. It also helped to get the cause of better planning noticed, though it would take many years even for the best to really take this on board.

The employer brand perspective made for a strong point of view and impressed many clients. Even if the reality did not change much, it led to a string of high-profile wins that gave us confidence and attracted a new Managing Director for the recruitment advertising business – Simon Howard, then 32, who in time would become a serial recruitment entrepreneur. We won a competitive repitch for Tesco, then under the leadership of Ian McLaurin, his commercial director John Gildersleeve and a courageous HR Director, Leslie James, who together realised that Tesco's reputation needed to be built on the basis of its employees. That would not be done if, as a consultant's report had told them, the dominant culture was that of fear. Tesco's radical and positive change to its people management strategy started about 1987 and has been consistently followed ever since (see Tesco case study, Appendix 2).

What could I do to develop the vision? The problem was that the mass of clients we served were not at a level to buy anything more than immediate recruitment solutions, so the small consulting business in the division had to fend for itself. However, here was an area that should be able to lead the change to an upgraded, better researched and planned employment experience in place of a system that simply drummed up new cannon fodder to replace those who had left. As a result I recruited Bill Quirke, who after a 1st in English at Oxford and later business experience had joined the PR Company Burson Marstellar where he had been building an internal communications consulting practice. His problem there was that of being an add-on to the big PR fee earners who didn't then understand the importance of people at work. Our second need was to change the name of the consultancy to distinguish it from the mass recruitment and communications business and be better able to win its own work.

The name People in Business (PiB) was launched in January 1989. Despite some early successes, including a global assignment for Price Waterhouse and Project 2000 for the NHS, the new venture came under increasing pressure from a new group chairman, David Norman. David was a brisk, self-confident, warrior type leader focused on results rather than vision, and uncomfortable with the creative businesses he had taken on. He regarded my commitment to a soft issue business like PiB as an incorrect use of time and argued that we would make more money if I concentrated on the recruitment businesses. In May 1992 he suggested that we close PiB to achieve this, and we started a brief conversation that would set the course of my life from then on. I said that if he didn't believe in PiB why didn't I take it on, and we quickly agreed a deal in the next few days.

I had spoken on the subject of employer branding publicly for the first time at the UK's Chartered Institute of Personnel and Development conference at Harrogate in 1990 and again in 1991 at another CIPD event entitled *Building your Employer Brand*. In 1995 we decided to do some initial research on awareness and understanding and Tim Ambler, Research Fellow at London Business School, took on the project working with MBA students Christian Ingerslev and Andrew Wiseman. They talked to 27 leading employers and their HR, Marketing and communications people and the results were published in the *Journal of Brand Management* in 1996.[3] The results highlighted the following.

Language was an issue. The concept of the employer brand had not yet entered the lexicon of most HR and communications professionals, and there was some resistance to introducing marketing language to the HR discipline. Many of the respondents felt that the concept risked having some negative overtones, given their perception of marketing as artificial and manipulative. These comments demonstrated the gap that too often exists in the mutual understanding between HR and the marketing function.

While many of the respondents recognised the implicit existence of the concept, there was some resistance to recognising the employer brand as a separate and distinct approach. There was certainly some resistance to adding a further thought process to an already quite big schedule.

- 'We are doing very little to promote an employer brand within the firm. It is something we need to work on but I have more pressing issues.'
- 'Frankly we have so much to do at the moment that we just want to get the basics right. The employer brand concept is not essential.'

The above thought reminds me of the old line: 'I'll get on to marketing when sales pick up.'

Corporate performance was identified by several respondents as a key prerequisite for a strong employer brand:

- 'Reputation is important but you must be successful as a business in order to have a good employer brand. You have to perform.'
- 'It is difficult for us to build our employer brand because we have not had good performance during the past two years.'

There was a theme in this research that the employer brand was part of communications, something you could talk about when you were in good shape. At that time respondents did not necessarily extend the concept to recognise that they were talking about the employment experience as a whole. This defining feature of employer brand thinking would only emerge later.

There was widespread support for the idea that an effective employer brand approach required senior management commitment and close cooperation between top management, marketing and HR.

- 'The biggest obstacle for a successful employer brand is the lack of funding and buy-in from top management.'

Finally, many people recognised the value of bringing some of the disciplines of marketing into the HR functions. This included an emphasis on getting the product right (i.e. the whole employment experience), making use of segmentation and umbrella branding, using compensation within the context of other functional or psychological benefits, realising the importance of professional communications and developing the techniques of relationship marketing. The above represented advanced thinking for 1996 and nine years later there is still much to be done to make this a reality.

How did the employer brand concept, and the work Andrew Lambert, Sue Clemenson and others had put into it, impact on our new venture, People in Business? Buyers of consulting are generally focused on the solution of an immediate problem. In most cases we used the concept to provide a robust framework for tackling a wide range of more immediate issues to do with communications and relationships at work. One of the earliest tools we used in this context was the employer brand 'wheel', an early prototype of our employer brand mix tool (see Chapter 11), which lays out the key factors influencing employees' experience of the employer brand (Figure 1.1). This provided an excellent framework for facilitating

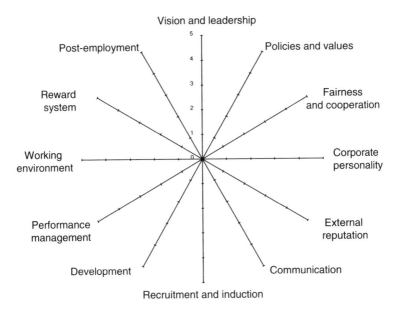

Figure 1.1 The employer brand 'wheel'. *Source*: PiB

workshops, prompting debate about the sort of organisation people currently experienced and, in turn, the kind of organisation they wanted to be. I recall a British Airways/British Airline Pilots Association session in 1999 at BALPA's office at Heathrow where the longstanding suspicion that can characterise management, union and flight crew relationships the world over, was put aside to debate what really matters if the flight crew employment experience is to be effective. The discussion brought out the reality of flying for BA and has always given me confidence flying behind a BA crew. The key elements were: trust in colleagues, the quality of training and training captains, the conduct of simulator testing and the quality of engineering and safety procedures. Of course rewards were an important dimension but nowhere near the profile that the press make out. High standards and mutual trust in colleagues was what flying for BA was really about from the pilot's perspective.

About the same time there was an event that demonstrated the size of gap that often exists between the customer and the employee-facing dimensions of most brands. That event was the short-lived appearance of a TV commercial for Sainsbury's. In the late 1990s Sainsbury's were concerned that shoppers believed that, for all Sainsbury's middle-class strengths in quality and service, their prices were higher than their leading competitors. This was galling because many of their prices were in fact highly competitive.

Sainsbury's marketing people therefore embarked on advertising which aimed to put this misconception right. They called it *'Something to shout about'*. Perfectly reasonable you might think. However, the problem came, as it so often does, in the execution. They wanted a high-profile presenter to talk in store with a member of staff about the real value they offered. I heard from someone on the agency team at the time that Ruby Wax was the favoured presenter, but for some reason she could not do it and John Cleese was hired. The script might have worked with Wax but with Cleese, at his Fawlty Towers best, the result was disastrous. The helpful and well meaning member of staff involved appeared to be totally belittled by Cleese's lecture on Sainsbury's pricing, and whatever the customer out-take, it caused uproar among Sainsbury's 140,000 people. This story was covered in the advertising press but dwelt on the future of their agency and marketing people. From our employer brand perspective, the real questions were:

- Did the Sainsbury's marketing people show the original treatment to anyone in HR, in internal communications or to store management?
- They obviously won approval for it from senior management, in which case did the latter even consider the potential effect on employees?
- During production did they test an animatic or later show the final film to any members of staff?

I do not know the answers to these questions, and the personnel of the time and their suppliers have all left the stage – some earlier than others.

This avoidable commercial tragedy made me think how, in organisational development terms, it could have been avoided. I suspect those questions were not asked, indeed not even thought of being asked, and the silo mentality had gained another scalp.

In October 2000 I introduced the role and job description of the Employer Brand Manager in a talk I gave to the Association of Graduate Recruiters. We will return to this subject in Chapter 11. However, given the above horror story, it is worth mentioning one of the first companies to appoint an Employer Brand Manager – it was Sainsbury's.

The Changing Needs and 2
Aspirations of Employees

On the face of it you might believe that employer brand thinking had only become relevant for major employers since McKinsey's 'War for Talent' and many similar papers that have highlighted the difficulty of recruiting and retaining capable people.[1]

There are many current pressures today which encourage employers to treat their people with the same care and coherence as they would value customers. However, the demands for good employer brand management have always been with us when expectations of a workforce have been extreme. In seeking examples of those conditions one has only to look at military history. Biographers of Wellington have always highlighted his support for his troops and his determination to move forward only when the necessary logistics were in place. His famous words in the aftermath of Waterloo: 'The next greatest misfortune to losing a battle is to gain such a victory as this', reflects his humanity.[2] Montgomery in 1943 told his 220,000 men in the desert: 'When all this is over and they ask you what you did in the war you need only say I was in the Eighth Army.'[3] Like Wellington he was trusted not to risk his forces unnecessarily and, on his deathbed, wondered what the 13,000 killed at Alamein were going to think of him. That concern plus his surefooted strategic ability and independence, earned him extraordinary loyalty. This year is the 200th anniversary of Trafalgar and the same values, as well as brilliance, created the loyalty of sailors to Lord Nelson. Many of the great employer brands of the past were military ones.

Most employees over the centuries have been agricultural labourers, and, for most of the industrial revolution, unskilled workers, with the pressure to perform being the pressure to eat. Capital, in the form of employers, needed labour of the most basic kind, whether hard manual work or repetitive machine minding. While there were much publicised exceptions, like the early Quaker entrepreneurs, human resources were plentiful, expendable and cheap. An extreme example of this was the debate among British plantation owners in the Caribbean in the late eighteenth century on the optimum way of managing sugar production. Which was more profitable: To look after slaves well in the belief that their productivity and longevity would show a greater return, or to work them intensively and then simply replace them with new 'saltwater' slaves? It was against inhuman calculations like these that Wilberforce and Buxton had to fight for so long to end the British slave trade in 1807 and the actual ownership of slaves across the British Empire in 1834. The interests of slave owners were powerfully represented at Westminster and the status quo has proved a formidable rampart for employment reformers to this day. Just consider what was said in opposition to the idea of a UK minimum wage in 1999. The CBI thought then that £4.40 was too high a level and would have 'a very serious impact on jobs and inflation'.[4]

One only has to read of the slow grudging pace of change in some of the UK's major employers to see how recently a very different balance between capital and labour existed. It isn't just Orwell's description of coal mining in *The Road to Wigan Pier* in the 1930s.[5] The American writer Clancy Sigal, writing about mining in the 1960s in *Weekend in Dinlock*, told the same story 30 years later,[6] as did D.H. Lawrence in his description of a local mining village in *Lady Chatterley's Lover*: 'The people were as haggard, shapeless and dreary as the countryside, and as unfriendly . . . Gulf impassable . . . breach indescribable.'[7] It is not surprising that, in the early 1990s, William Woodruff's *Road to Nab End* – about his upbringing in the cotton town of Blackburn in the 1920s – became such a recent bestseller.[8] It struck a nerve for anyone with a childhood in the North (including mine). The unrelenting pressures of mill work and life in damp rented houses remain in the DNA for millions. T.S. Eliot's poem *The Waste Land*, describing city workers crossing London Bridge ('I had not thought death had undone so many'), expressed a similar blankness among white-collar workers.[9] Consider Arthur Miller's line in *Death of a Salesman* when Willie Loman, the long-serving salesman of the title, is dismissed: 'You can't eat the orange and throw the peel away. A man is not a piece of fruit.'[10] John Steinbeck, Sinclair Lewis and Clifford Odets all captured the same sentiments about the oppression and drudgery of work.

What have been the forces for change? Let us start with the Unions. While for much of my lifetime UK Unions have been seen as some of the major forces of conservatism, their ability to represent working people and drive change to achieve collective bargaining, health and safety improvements, paid holidays and improved consultation achieved extraordinary reforms in the period 1890–1960. Organised labour made sure that employers had at least to address the basics, and that has now largely been achieved. The future role of Unions remains uncertain, as the declining membership over many years demonstrates, but they can still pack a punch within some of our more traditional public sector services. Organised labour, representing a precious and hard to achieve skill, remains a powerful force. Just think of the Law Society, the British Medical Association (representing 193,000 British doctors) and the British Airline Pilots Association (representing 9000 flight crew members). These are heavyweight bodies and, at their best, they can do much more than simply protect the historic status quo. They can play their part in changing it for the better as well as helping to set standards and offer personal guidance to members. If they do this they should still have a significant role to play in shaping the employment experience.

While I would like to think that many employers have now recognised the benefit of valuing their employees as much as they value their customers, I fear that that is not necessarily accepted standard practice. Most managers may nod to it, but what has made Employer Brand management important is a host of other forces that have little to do with the accepted management rhetoric on the subject. Beware the CEO who uses pat phrases like 'People are our greatest asset', before moving on to the numbers.

For a start, technological innovation has changed what employees are needed to do. Unskilled manual work represents only 18% of UK employees. The vast majority do have some technical skill which, however modest, is transportable. Of course, there may be too many people with the same skills and those skills can become out of date. Adrian Furnham, Professor of Psychology at Birkbeck, tells a story about his father, at one time one of Fleet Street's finest, a linotype operator doing a highly skilled, sometimes dangerous, job of creating slugs of type from hot metal to form the basis of rotary letterpress newspaper production. When journalists started to input their own copy directly, the need for that skill disappeared. In London, in the early 1980s, linotype operators were gone within three years.

With the emergence of individual skills has come the need for improved delegation and therefore empowerment. Business life today is too complex to put the time into intense supervision or to micro manage other people's work. As a result, a greater need for trust in employees is critical, once they know what to do, the standards that are expected, and what they can do without recourse to management.

Alongside the technical skills expected in most jobs today comes a need for customer service and the presence of sufficient emotional intelligence in dealing with other people, either as internal or external customers. It is difficult to think of any area today where some level of customer service skill is not required. However, I do remember that London Transport's research into the recruitment of bus drivers revealed that one of the reasons for wanting to drive the famous London Routemaster double-decker bus was that the driver was only expected to drive. As the Routemasters have been replaced by Single Operator buses, this has had to change to some extent but the interaction between driver and customer is still very limited. It is worth noting that there is also a lengthy waiting list for the drivers of London Underground trains, where the separation from customers is even more complete.

Let us now consider the power of personal expectations. In the early 1960s I remember William Deedes, then a Conservative Minister, speaking to an Advertising conference in Brighton. Deedes asked the conference to consider the impact of new minorities with which we would have to become increasingly concerned. They were: 'parents distanced from and eclipsed by their ambitious and high-performing children', 'those adults who did not have saleable skill' and, sadly, what he bluntly called 'the stupid child'. He said: 'Never has it been less fun to be a stupid child than today' given the expectation that most of your contemporaries would be taking public exams, with the course set for A-Levels and University entrance. Since those days, of course, the opportunities for non-academic subjects has been increased and the negative effect of being unable to compete on classic subjects has been lessened. While self-esteem may have been preserved in this way, the modern job market continues to make sure that the truth will out.

Many people at work today have been active CV builders and career planners from an early stage. They know that they must attain transportable skills; they know that they must push themselves and assess the competition. They have done their homework on themselves, and their career management is more likely to be based on realism than simply aspiration.

Finally, employees are becoming increasingly litigious. Employees are now more confident and better able to afford professional advice when they believe they have been treated unfairly.

This form of litigation is surely less likely to happen when the culture of the organisation enables people to express themselves more openly. Our experience indicates that when employees are given more control over their working conditions they also perform better. Provided that people are given suitable standards and guidelines, there is also less need for centralised control. As somebody who had to manage people in an advertising agency, these are lessons that any leader in that field must learn fast. Winston Fletcher's book *Creative People*[11] is required reading and a few years ago a *Harvard Business Review* article entitled 'How to Manage Millionaires' came to similar conclusions.[12] You have to find ways of getting powerful and independent people to make a contribution and you do that through recognition, peer group pressure and the desire of the individual to be associated with a group he or she truly rates. What millionaire wants to be seen to be letting down colleagues in a well-known charity? As a result, they are prepared to work very hard. Of course, most employees are like that, whether or not they are millionaires. Financial rewards are only important if they are out of line with what is seen as the appropriate rate for the job. Of those interviewed by NOP in 2004, 43% thought that job content was the main motivator in the workplace.[13] Only 14% noted pay as the key influence. For the umpteenth time in nearly 20 years of studying the workplace, the number one failure in this report was lack of recognition and poor communication. What is particularly uncomfortable from that survey is that while 50% of employers claimed that employee satisfaction was important to them, only 6% actually considered it as a major business priority.

The need for proper recognition lies deep in most of us. Time and again PiB's occupational psychologist John Toplis has revealed the deeply felt desire of people to receive personal recognition from those they are close to. When a former colleague of Crispin Davies, now Chief Executive of Reed Elsevier, said he ran the group as if he had a point to prove, it was probably because he came from a high-performing family (one brother at the top of McKinsey, another a partner at Freshfields, and another a High Court Judge). That works at all levels too. Remember Jack Ruby, the man who shot Lee Harvey Oswald? When he was sitting in the Dallas courtroom he said to the court artist: 'Gimme a little dignity will ya?'

The ability to deliver appropriate recognition to others demands so-called soft skills both interpersonal and intrapersonal. 'Interpersonal' means leading, communicating, influencing and working as a team but 'intrapersonal' actions are what count because they are all about my relationship with you and vice versa. Understanding *my* personal motivation, helping *me* solve *my* problem, helping *me* manage *myself*, that's when soft skills demonstrate their worth and are critical to an environment where flexibility, payment for results and great customer service are what counts. That means that bosses must be coaches and be able to generate greater recognition and greater trust.

The demand for recognition takes us on to the delicate subject of work–life balance. One of the prolific Winston Fletcher's latest books is entitled *Beating the 24/7*, in which he draws on interviews with a number of successful people such as Sir Christopher Bland, Richard Branson, Dennis Stevenson, Sarah Hogg and Nicola Horlick.[14] They all have sensible and pleasant things to say about a properly balanced life, and have all been highly successful from their early days. I suspect that achieving an appropriate work–life balance for yourself is a function of brain power, planning, delegation and focus. Perhaps some of the people Winston writes about have actually had to do the occasional 24/7, but it was a special occasion. That is very different to what drives most work–life balance commentators, which is the unrelenting long-hours culture within some organisations (magic circle law firms, for example). A TUC official (who spoke to Catharine Barnard, Senior Lecturer in Law, and Simon Deakin, Professor of Corporate Governance, both at Cambridge) thought that removing the EC opt out on long hours would have little impact in the case of white-collar workers 'because you are talking about ingrained overtime cultures that are not pay driven'.

In any case, the working time directive is both complex and poorly enforced. As a result it has not had enough force to counter the UK's long-hours culture, and we believe that a prime opportunity to encourage businesses to rethink inefficient working practices has been lost.

While overtime payments are critical to many people's ability to maintain their current standard of living, it is interesting to note from an Investors in People survey in August 2004 that 32% of all working women believe that work–life balance is something that employers should deliver for them.[15] As British Airways at Heathrow found out to their cost, interfering with the measurement of check-in staff was not a function of money, it was the need to manage childcare arrangements. The work–life balance, thanks to considerable government and private sector support (e.g. Employers for Work*life* Balance), has raised the profile of this subject and it would be hard to develop the employer brand of any organisation that did not have a firm point of view on this issue, however complex the underlying aspects are. One of them is the pressure of *work–work* balance as opposed to work–life balance i.e. when a low basic hours agreement has been reached, allowing time for employees to engage in other forms of economic activity. Air traffic controllers and firefighters have often been mentioned in this context.

What else do employer brand creators have to concern themselves with in 2005? We should certainly mention growing inequality on both sides of the Atlantic. In 1980 the average US CEO was paid around 40 times as much as the average worker, now the multiple is over 400.[16] While the UK and the USA have been able to demonstrate significant levels of social mobility, the Cato Institute study of marriage patterns[17] may be putting this movement at risk since, as *The Economist* puts it in the same article, 'yuppies marry yuppies these days'. Small wonder, perhaps, since so many people today are working in ghettos composed of nothing else but people with similar educational achievements and aspirations. Furthermore, the children from those marriages are likely to perpetuate that lack of mobility by joining high-performance parts of the private sector from private education. In the UK, it is not just Oxford and Cambridge who have a weighting to those from private education far greater than the average. You can also add Edinburgh, Durham, Newcastle, Sussex, Bristol, Manchester and several others, all of which have undergraduates from private education, and supposedly comprise a vastly greater percentage of the student body compared with the national average of 8% of all UK children. Just as this volume must affect the culture, values and behaviours of these universities, so it may do when these people move into the workplace, and employer brand management needs to consider how a truly inclusive culture is going to be built, given such a range of raw material.

Finally, any chapter entitled 'Changing needs and aspirations of employees' must address the fundamental question of whether highly skilled people really want to work for large corporations. Many argue that while big firms are great places to start, they are not where you want to end up, and it is a shorter step to doing it on your own than it has been in the past. A client at one of the leading hedge funds, Man Investments, recently drew our attention to the large number of ambitious young people setting up new firms in this area over recent years.

As Daniel Goleman[18] said: 'There was a long period of managerial domination of the corporate hierarchy when the manipulative, jungle fighter boss was rewarded. But that rigid hierarchy started breaking down in the 1980s under the twin pressures of globalisation and information technology.' The jungle fighter symbolises where the corporation has been; the virtuoso in interpersonal skills is the corporate future.

In this chapter I have tried to cover what we believe are the prime influences on people at work today and these demand real understanding of them by anyone wishing to build an effective employer brand.

Investors Awaken 3

In the previous chapter we showed the pressures on employer brand builders in coping with some of the new factors that are demanding improved employment practice if people of the right quality are going to be successfully recruited, retained and engaged. While the areas for consideration are many, any writer specialising in people at work matters could have written a similar call to arms at any time in the past 30 years.

Why have more of them not been addressed? It's an important question because any new approach, such as the employer brand, needs to assess why it is that so many people-related ideas do not seem to attract the necessary firepower. It isn't just the CIPD; look at any conference operator's mail shot and spot an area that speakers have not been covering in one way or another for years.

The purpose of this chapter is to review what we believe is going to be the major change agent for the people-management business – and that involves the investment community and the shareholders whose funds it invests. Just as the US President Calvin Coolidge once memorably said 'The business of America is business', it is the same gut feeling that drives the way things work world wide. Ultimately, business and commercial thinking drive what matters at work, influenced by the ego, ambitions, hopes and fears of the senior executives responsible. No HR best practice papers ever become reality if they are not linked in to these core drivers.

I am indebted to Jeremy van den Arend, an ex-HRD of Reed Elsevier, for this thought on the promotion records of Navy versus Army leaders which demonstrates the historically greater importance of physical assets rather than people. Historically, the Navy made the tough decisions on promotion early while the Army made the tough decisions after an action. The rationale was that command in the Navy obviously involved a significant capital investment (i.e. a ship) and that was something of much greater importance in the historic scheme of things than the military personnel involved. Senior army officers did get fired for actions that were unsuccessful and often incurred an unacceptable loss of life, but there was a greater likelihood that they would have been *given* a greater chance to fail.

That story is relevant because, if the people aspects of business life are as critical as we believe them to be, then how they are managed in the context of an organisation's commercial plan should be a touchstone for investors.

Historically, people issues have only grabbed investors attention when there is a serious disagreement at senior level. That could be over future strategy but equally likely a disagreement over some cultural or chemistry fit around who should do what job and how. The other big issue was a crippling strike in an area where no alternative labour was available. I recall the near strike of British Airways flight crew in August 1996. It didn't actually happen but that potential event lost the airline £15 million in bookings in the preceding three weeks.

Those two risk areas (senior management disagreement or a strike threat) pose an immediate risk to both earnings and the external perception of the firm in the eyes of investors. Most of what we were discussing in the previous chapter is on a longer time frame, but there is evidence that investors are getting their minds round the importance of employment issues.

We will review these factors:

- Realisation that the causes of commercial failure often lie not only in management's strategic ability but in their ability as employers.
- Pressure to change the way the investment community works.
- US, European and UK legislation on compliance and governance.
- Growing awareness among employees of their rights and the threat of litigation.
- And, finally, the pressures from line and marketing management demanding a more effective approach to improve the productivity and attractiveness of the employment experience. Just notice how often the employee subject comes up in brand and marketing literature.

Management must be able to demonstrate to investors that it has the employment experience well planned, delivered and measured and are seen to be doing so by analysts and media commentators. Those demands cannot be met by the occasional piece of good news management cherry-picked from across the company; it needs a coherent, coordinated and constantly measured approach, hence the relevance of employer brand management and the demand for regular assessment it brings.

We will look first at the causes of commercial failure due to management's ability as an employer. Having been involved as a consultant in over 30 mergers and acquisitions from a relationship and communication standpoint, I can recall many examples where deals have failed to reach their objectives because the employment aspects have not received the necessary attention.

However, one case stands out where I was involved not as a consultant but as a senior executive. That was the offer for sale and simultaneous acquisition represented by the old Charles Barker Group, the substantial advertising and communications business, when it bought the headhunters Norman Broadbent and, at the same time, went public in 1986. Charles Barker was then the second largest UK-owned communications group with pre-tax trading profits of £2.6 million on a turnover of £136.6 million. Recognising the profitability and opportunity of HR led the firm to buy the well-known executive search company Norman Broadbent. They, too, had had a remarkable record, making £1 million profit on turnover of £3.3 million in 1985. That had been achieved by a staff of just 18 in London and 4 in Hong Kong and demonstrated the extraordinary profitability of a significant search company at its peak. Putting the two companies together provided a combined firm with proforma tax profits of £3.6 million on revenue of £83 million. Given that record, investors rapidly took up 25% of the equity on 21 May 1986.

With the benefit of hindsight and nearly 20 years in the study of successful employment practices, why would a combined firm with such a sparkling record run into the sand a few years later? At least the surviving entity, now BNB Resources plc, still trades and much has been done by the present management to bring the business back into the black. However, the shares, after numerous dilutions, are only a fraction of the 150 p price at flotation.

Against the remarkable promise of the IPO, why did it fail? After all, the strategic provision of joined-up advertising, communications and HR was advanced thinking. Furthermore, the businesses had some massive talents as numerous ex-Charles Barker entrepreneurs have demonstrated: Angela Heylin, Angus Maitland and Piers Pottinger in public relations and Paddy Murray in Sales Promotion, to name but a few. Additionally, London remains full of successful Charles Barker alumni: Michael Prideaux has been responsible for BAT's external relations for many years and Alan, now Lord, Watson, chairs WPP's Burson-Marstellar. The Norman Broadbent business has generated a plethora of independent businesses, among them Richard Boggis-Rolfe at Odgers, Julian Sainty of Sainty Hird and Miles Broadbent has emerged as the Miles Partnership. It should have worked brilliantly and the reason for its failure lay in the management of the employment experience.

To begin with, there was nothing remotely approaching a human resource management system. There was no HR executive advising on how best to manage over 700 people. When you reflect how mercurial, egotistical, insecure and greedy advertising and communication people can be (let alone headhunters), that was a grievous error.

Of course, a culture of new business winning, publicity, profitability and rewards does not necessarily engender a culture of thought. There was no employee research of any kind. Perhaps if there had been (for example, one of the independent qualitative studies of the type in which PiB specialises), there would have been a way of putting the truth on the table and harnessing the joint energies of very different people to address the issues that would undoubtedly have emerged. The historic culture also had a role to play. It was what I would call 'Old City' where skills and personal rewards were infinitely more important than management. That was left for lesser mortals and was reflected in the leadership. All four chairmen over a period of 30 years, from 1970 to 2000, reflected that culture – Kyrle Simond, Julian Wellesley, Antony Snow and David Norman. All of them business developers and instinctive recruiters of good people (though no psychological testing of recruits was ever done) but none of them with training or enthusiasm for good HR management as it is known today, and with David Norman being the only one with any formal business education (a Harvard MBA). I recall, for example, that no training ever took place other than on two occasions, with the importation of a New York consultant on winning pitches and, at another session, a time management guru.

Finally, despite occasional off sites in luxurious country house hotels there was insufficient clarity on the role of and respect for the group centre. What value did it add to the businesses? It was always difficult to answer that question because everyone in the senior management was 99% driven by the needs of managing their own patch. There were no stated central values and few group activities that pulled people together. A combination of advertising, public relations, sales promotion and head-hunting rapidly became an explosive mixture. That mixture was ignited, as so often happens, by two potential and heavyweight corporate discussions, neither of which resulted in a deal. The first, in August 1988, was with Martin Sorrell and his then finance director Robert Lerwill of WPP; the second was with Peter Gummer (now Lord Chadlington), then chairman of Shandwick. These would have been handsome solutions had they happened.

The impact of the failure of both these potential corporate changes resulted in the eventual break up of a group that had been taken public so recently and so confidently. This story demonstrates that commercial failure can be directly linked to a firm's ability as an employer, however sound the strategy and the technical abilities of the people.

The second factor for review is the way the investment community has tended to work and the extent to which it is taking notice of 'people issues' in fund manager assessments today. If skills in managing the employment experience become more critical, then it should follow that the investment community should be demanding a much more rigorous approach to this aspect in its assessment. Historically, the City has worked on a short-term basis and has limited its assessment from an HR point of view to what it thinks of the Chief Executive and his/her finance director. What has their recent record been in terms of financial performance? The provenance of that attitude lies deep in the history of the UK financial services community. *The Economist* stated in Sir Alistair Morton's obituary in September 2004: 'Although he read law at Oxford he had not otherwise brushed with the British establishment until he met it in the city and in government. He never got used to its arrogant, duplicitous, so-polite ways.'[1] For Sir Alistair Morton read 'generations of business leaders with the same view', because people who have entered the financial community seldom have any working experience of industry and commerce. They respect their own skills rather than that of professional management and, although they have every intention of earning substantial rewards, have no particular desire to manage great City businesses. That, of course, is a convenient view because there are hardly any substantial City businesses that remain in UK ownership. American, German, Swiss, French and Japanese personnel not only own the major firms in the City but also hold senior management jobs. As long as the owners still reward skilled Brits for doing what they do well, that seems to be fine with the latter.

The above conditions are not favourable ground for taking a more rigorous look at the effect of the employment experience on future financial performance. This means spending more time on analysis. A few years ago we had to assess the views of City analysts on attitudes to a recently announced strategy by the management of a FTSE company. My colleagues and I were amazed by the range of companies that these so-called specialists had to cover within the group of categories for which they were responsible. They certainly had no time to work in any depth and the information on which they made their judgements had to be accessible and immediately relevant.

Yet consider the pressures to get more involved. According to the National Bureau of Economic Research, 32% of the market value of the top 500 US firms in 1982 consisted of 'intangible assets' – the intellectual and human capital that an organisation creates and possesses.[2] By 2001, it had moved to being more than 85%. Given that importance, who can dispute that competence in managing relationships is anything other than a competitive advantage? Shell's damaging error concerning its estimates of oil reserves reflected an employee relationship, values and behaviours issue at its heart.

Signs that senior line managers and HR people are good at creating the organisational structure must surely be a key sign of excellence and future worth. The Oxford/Cornell Centre for advanced Human Resource studies reflects the sort of initiatives that are raising the profile of this thinking.

Similarly, Accenture has published evidence that moving between large-scale recruitment and redundancies is enormously expensive.[3] They calculated that it cost £9bn to cut and subsequently refill the jobs of 789,000 people made redundant in the UK between 2001 and 2003. Yet how does the fund manager recognise the benefits of a firm holding its workforce together and not making the short-term cuts that the rest of the market may be doing?

The last five years have seen pressures on the financial community to take a broader view incorporating the employment aspects of commercial performance. In 2000 the DTI asked Paul Myners, former chairman of Gartmore Investment management, to produce a report on the City's relationship with the organisations in which it invests.[4] Chapter 5 of that report spells out the demands that fund managers should be making of the firms in which they invest. Rather than sell and walk away, they should mix in.

After all, they look after £2500 billion for domestic and overseas clients both institutional and retail. In the US it is £18.5 trillion under management but how active are they? Myners says: 'the most powerful argument for intervention in a company is financial self-interest'. He goes on to argue that the fund manager's clients have the right to expect them to know when they will intervene, how they will do so and 'how they will measure effectiveness'. Significantly, Myners notes that they may need to augment their skill base and communication processes to do this. Dead right, but they cannot do this by looking only at historic numbers! Surely they need to demand wider indicators on future performance, including the answers to tough questions on HR matters, which we will cover later in this chapter.

Overall, Paul Myners called on shareholders to challenge bad management more vigorously. In particular, he urged them to question the disparity between top executive salaries and those below them, and link senior pay with average salary growth within the company rather than with that of executives in other companies. Shareholders should also play a role in the nomination and selection of non-executive directors. In 2004 there was a graphic example of this when Sainsbury's desire to appoint a chosen chairman was successfully blackballed by investors.

In February 2003 the Government commissioned a task force under Denise Kingsmill, then deputy chair of the Competition Commission, to issue guidelines on how quoted companies might report on the subject of 'human capital' – essentially how organisations generate value from their employees.[5] Kingsmill argued that annual reports might contain details on size and constituents of the workforce, retention and motivation of employees, skills and competencies necessary, training needs, remuneration, fair employment practices, leadership and succession. However, it stopped short of proposing any specific measurements. Today, the Accounting Standards Board is still considering the content of operating and financial reviews and is awaiting the result of a working party on what they should contain. It will be interesting to see what HR measures emerge. Commentators have noted that this working party contained no one with experience in HR.

In our experience as consultants, often with large and sophisticated firms, online human capital information is often difficult to obtain. That must mean that human capital metrics are not studied regularly by senior management. The second hurdle, having gathered material on a regular basis, is the challenge of publishing it. In our view good companies will publish because positive statistics in the employment area must increase the profile of the firm for recruiters, advisers and candidates. One has only to look at the great popularity of league tables within employment to see the use that firms make of good scores. The *Financial Times* and *The Sunday Times* annual assessments are well supported (though mostly by small to medium-sized companies), and I know how proud one of our clients is to be regularly featured. Hiscox, the insurance group, has been placed tenth and eleventh in two of the last three years. Not only does this reflect the truth (in our view) about an outstanding company but it has given Hiscox management greater confidence in making its culture, and the way it manages its people is one of the most distinctive aspects of the company.

In early 2005 I was a judge on the assessment of 100 companies selected for a book entitled *Britain's Top Employers*, published by Corporate Research Foundation and *The Guardian*.[6] For the first time, under pressure from judges like me and others, the book has a quantified element; an independent assessment formed from 10 dimensions. These include pay and benefits, opportunities for promotion, training and development, opportunities for travel and international work, company culture, the firm's ability to innovate, diversity and equal opportunities, social responsibility, corporate governance and its environmental record. Note that these 10 dimensions do not include the ability to make money! Surely anyone judging a firm as a place to work is going to want to know the answer to that? However, the publishers argue that if you get the right people and the right strategy throughout the firm, as well as at the top, the rest should follow. Indeed, just look at WPP's mission statement.

You would think that it would be something along the lines of 'helping our clients to achieve growth in sales and profits, etc.'. But look at what comes first. The WPP mission in its 2003 report[7] reads as follows:

> *Our mission: to develop and manage talent; to apply that talent, throughout the world, for the benefit of clients; to do so in partnership; to do so with profit.*

WPP know that if they don't get the right people they haven't got a business.

Finally, there is the pressure on senior teams to improve their general effectiveness. This has resulted in the work conducted by Sir Derek Higgs on corporate governance.[8] The combined code on corporate governance stated that a listed company should 'undertake a formal and rigorous annual evaluation of its performance and its committees and individual directors'. Given the corporate failures in recent years highlighting the shortcoming of boards whose directors failed to safeguard shareholders' interest, surely few can object to the principles of evaluation. However, recent studies have shown that there is some way to go before undertaking these assessments becomes the norm. What will provide more formal implementation (and faster) will be the fear that, in the event of a firm being under pressure on a performance matter, if the assessments of the senior people were not in fact done, what action resulted? If anyone has doubts about this, just study a Government accident investigation report. When someone is killed or seriously injured, the resulting Health and Safety Executive report is an impressive and reassuring document covering every aspect of the technical and human process issues leading up to the tragedy. While financial failure is not usually associated with death or injury, it can nevertheless be a human tragedy for millions of investors and we are moving, correctly, to an environment where financial failure can expect the same rigorous and far-ranging questions on why it happened.

In the past, Health and Safety accident reports often concluded that technical failure was a cause. As someone now with quite a long experience in the world of flight crew, I read the late Sir Miles Thomas's autobiography *Out on a Wing*.[9] When he was chairman of BOAC he had to cope with no less than five total hull losses of BOAC aircraft. Mechanical and engineering failure were considered responsible for four of them. Now, of course, you could argue that the engineers, planners, testers and other experts responsible for creating and approving the material that went into the aircraft failed if their work resulted in tragedy, so that by the severest measures almost all accidents, other than the result of an Act of God, are the result of human failure. However, the design, construction and systems in a modern aircraft are infinitely more reliable than they were 50 years ago and, as a result, flying incidents today are most often the result of direct human failure, i.e. pilot error or, occasionally, air traffic control.

The news of the failure of fund management in recent years was the lead story in *The Daily Telegraph* on 31 May 2003.[10] It highlighted the news that the FTSE had fallen at its lowest to 50% of its all-time high, resulting in black holes for many major pension holders. The initiatives and ideas we have described so far in this chapter are part of an expectation that a major readjustment of how fund managers work is required. One result has, of course, been the rise of the hedge fund. I sometimes wonder how members of the human resource community would perform as fund managers. Would people with a real grasp of the culture, processes, structure, relationships and leadership of an organisation be in a better position to assess whether they were involved with success or failure? Would they be in a better qualified to spot the crispness and demanding tension that you find within a well-managed business?

To help fund managers to prepare for such an assessment we have provided the following list of possible questions and expected answers.

1. Reputation as an employer

What is unique about your offer to good people?

Expect a decisive and research-based reply.

Your alumni. Can you name people who have left you and gone on to great success?

Expect names. All good employers should be great springboards.

What is your conversion rate of job offers to acceptance?

A good answer is 75%+.

2. Leadership

How many of the senior executive group were internal promotions versus external recruitment?

Expect a balance. If they're mostly external what succession planning has been done?

Is your most senior HR professional in the top team?

Expect yes.

Would he/she be an insider if you were considering an acquisition?

If not, why not?

If the organisation is a multinational, is the diversity of the company broadly represented within the executive group?

The answer should be yes. If not, there should be a good reason.

How do you lead/manage change?

Look for evidence of well-managed projects where employee views have been consulted and well briefed.

Would any number of staff be able to tell me the goals of the organisation?

Expect yes (then ask: how do you know?).

How are senior management decisions communicated?

Expect regular face-to-face (not just emails/newsletters/videos).

3. Communications

What do you do to ensure that people at all levels are aware of performance and profitability issues?

Look for a regular system of team briefing with links to the organisation's performance.

How do you promote line of sight with the customer?

Look for managed themes in their internal communication.

What feedback systems do you have?

Expect more than ad hoc, i.e. clear process on down, up and across.

What sharing mechanism do you have to spread corporate expertise and reduce dependence on key players?

Expect rigorous mechanisms.

When was your last employee survey?

Should have been in last year.

What was the response rate?

Probe if the answer is below 75%.

How were the results fed back?

Should be face-to-face process where people were involved with local action-planning.

What action did you take in response to key findings after it was complete?

Expect a specific response, i.e. 'still considering' is a bad answer, surveys reports should identify clear areas for action.

If you don't do surveys how do you get feedback?

Should be specific, processes articulated.

4. Values
What are the values of your company?
How were the values created?

*Expect an immediate and succinct answer of 4/5 statements.
The wrong answer is 'by the management'. Values should be rooted in reality and have been identified and agreed with employees.*

How are they hard–wired into the organisation?

Should have tangible structures, processes, etc., e.g. performance management.

Are they reflected in people's behaviour?

Expect concise answer on communications, clarity, customer service.

(Supplementary) How do you know that?

Staff survey, appraisal reviews and feedback from training.

5. Employee relations
How many Industrial Tribunal cases have you had in the last year? What is the trend?

Expect a quantified answer.

What were the results?

Probe if any tribunals have been lost and why.

How many potential Industrial Tribunals have been settled before an appearance?

Likely to be higher than those actually processed through a hearing.

Do you recognise a union(s)? If so, when did you recognise it? What are your relations like? When do you talk to them? Do you have a partnership agreement?

Worry if it is a recent recognition. In a long-term relationship there should be a partnership agreement and they should be meeting informally and/or regularly outside formal bargaining meetings.

What are your sickness/absence figures compared to competitors?

Expect under 5 days per year per head.

6. Compensation

What percentage of total costs are people related? (And how does that relate to the competition?)

Investigate if higher than competition.

What quartile does your compensation policy aim for?

Expect a well-reasoned answer.

7. Staff turnover

What is your turnover compared to your competitors?

Retail at shop floor level will be 35% +. Financial service average is 18%. They should know their competitors and their own numbers.

Have you detected any pattern in your exit interviews? Are exit interviews analysed across the organisation? What are you doing to address retention?

Expect a clear answer on why good people leave and what is being done about it.

We now move to the third factor, which is increasing attention on the management of the employment experience – that is, the volume of US, European and UK legislation on compliance and governance. While the pressure on management is one of performance, the wall of new compliance legislation reflects a much more invasive influence.

The new internal control disclosure requirements arising, for example, from Sarbanes-Oxley place public responsibility with management regarding the effectiveness of internal controls.[11] These are certain over the years to influence the organisational culture, the importance of quality, control and risk management structures and we know how burdensome the influence of these new demands are not just for finance directors and their staffs but also for Human Resource executives.

Note the Accounting Standards Board recommendations on performance measures when they say that those used internally and those reported on to external stakeholders 'should not be radically different'.[12] Furthermore, the company should focus on measuring and reporting their main value drivers rather than getting the right figure to satisfy market expectations. However sensible this sounds, it presents a real challenge for many excellent businesses we know. Yet good management information, in particular on people, should be the backbone for all strategic planning. Lack of quality information has undoubtedly been responsible for poor decisions, and these errors tend to happen when roles, relationships and the culture get in the way of good behaviour and communication. One has only to think of the extraordinary tale within the previous management of Marks & Spencer's when a commentator said that negative customer research information was withheld from the Chief Executive of the time! Similarly, reading Bill Vlasic and Bradley Stertz's blockbuster on the Daimler Chrysler transaction, published in 2000, it was telling to see how ramshackle the Human Resource judgements were.[13] I have rarely read a more painful tale of the impact of ego, ambition and pride running roughshod over good practice. So often the financial, political and market pressures cause dreadful employment decisions to be made.

I know, because I have been there. I recall in my advertising days coping with the loss of a major account, Anchor Butter. We had created a famous campaign but changes in New Zealand resulted in a review that we lost. While the agency was profitable and in good overall shape, and Anchor only responsible for 10% of our income, I overreacted and encouraged the board to buy a small competitor I had come across which would, at a stroke, add that income back and provide the post-loss fillip I, like all senior managers, would like to demonstrate. It was a disaster. The team we bought were miles away from the hard disciplines we had built and the business that they brought was flaky. Within a year both people and business had largely gone. How much better it would have been to have taken a steadier, longer term and more truly confident stance. While the stakes at Chrysler or Daimler-Benz were in billions, I truly understand the pressures to cut corners on human resource matters even though, at the time, deep down you know you are doing it. The influence of governance and compliance is to make opportunistic 'get out of trouble' action less likely and more unforgivable.

It is not, of course, simply investors and legislators who are putting pressure on management. While they may have awoken to the need for better management of the employment experience, so too have employees themselves. As they become more skilled, more mobile and more confident and, in particular, when paid very well, they become more demanding and litigious. In the past year there have been numerous high-profile cases involving sex discrimination and unfair dismissal in the City. These employees knew their rights, took first-class legal advice and had the confidence to go for it. These much publicised cases were probably the tip of the iceberg; hundreds more will have been resolved before going to court.

It is not only in the world of high-priced City workers that a new awareness of rights exists. Last year, according to the UK's Trades Union Council (TUC), three in five workers now complain of being stressed at work, with stress-related absence accounting for an estimated 6.5 million working days lost per year.[14] In addition, 6428 companies were forced to pay damages for workplace stress with an average payment of £51,000 – a 12-fold increase in the number of employees who successfully sued their employers in 2000. The TUC have reported that overload was the main cause of stress at work and their league table showed central government to be top of the list. You will have noted that we included the number of industrial tribunals and similar work-related disagreements in our list of questions for fund managers. I have long believed that there is a correlation between the number of cases requiring the advice of an employment lawyer and the quality of senior management in the organisation concerned.

Finally in this chapter let us look at the pressures within organisations from line and marketing management demanding a more effective approach to improve the productivity and attractiveness of the employment experience. Over the years I have observed that there is no greater pressure for HR people than that from colleagues to recruit quality people and to do so fast. For all the reasons we have covered in the book so far, line management and marketing people now seem well aware of how vital it is to recruit, retain and motivate the appropriate talent. That type of pressure is now so great that there are signs that, if Human Resources cannot deliver, line management will take it on themselves. We have argued in this chapter that the City's tectonic plates are moving and that investors are watching the management of the employment experience, and so are governments through tougher compliance regimes. The pressure that creates is now being felt by the Human Resource world and that is the subject for the next chapter – The People Management Challenge.

The People
Management Challenge

4

In October each year, The UK Chartered Institute of Personnel and Development (CIPD), the trade body of the HR world, invites its 125,000 members to an annual conference at Harrogate. About 2500 of these show up, making it the biggest commercial conference held in the UK. I first went to this event two weeks after starting my HR-facing career back in 1986. One of the themes in the conference that year, and it seems every year since, has been something along the lines of 'Whither HR?' or similar questions aiming to prompt discussions on the present and future role, the lack of power and what to do about it, whether or not the senior HR executive should be on the board of the organisation, etc., etc. Many of these questions are as unresolved now as they were then. Yet, as the preceding chapters in this book have argued, the need for powerful, professional, engaged HR executives has never been greater.

One of the bases on which this book has been created is that you cannot easily pick at one element that makes up the employment experience; you have to look at it in its entirety, just as you look at a brand in its entirety. However, it is interesting to see the effect that one well-timed and succinct expression of a major single issue has driven a change within the HR field. That was the *McKinsey Quarterly* in 1998 on 'The War for Talent',[1] in which this noble quote appeared:

> Companies are about to be engaged in a war for senior executive talent that will remain a defining characteristic of their competitive landscape for decades to come. Yet most are ill prepared and even the best are vulnerable.

Incidentally, note the selective nature of this opinion. While the headline 'The War for Talent' has been used in a general sense, in fact the real issue in McKinsey's view was for top talent. That may be true; certainly according to executive search people, but it actually impacts a much broader range of talent in an organisation. In the first quarter of 2005 there are recruitment challenges across a much wider range of levels and specialisms.

The impact this pressure is having is indicative of the need for change within HR itself. We are seeing quasi-marketing titles emerging like 'Director of Talent', 'Director of Recruitment Marketing', and 'People Director'. In a well-known American bank the creation of the graduate recruitment offer has been moved to the marketing function. In our experience the internal communications role tends to lie within Corporate Affairs rather than HR. Yet without HR's hands on the ropes of communications it restricts the function's day-to-day involvement with what actually happens in managing the action. Study the line up in *Acquisitions Monthly's* review of merger and acquisitions. You will see the name of the chief executive, the finance director, the bank, the lawyer and the communications agency – the latter being a critical ingredient not only in hostile bids but in the run up to an agreed transaction. While mergers and acquisitions are unique events they demonstrate what happens when the gloves are off, and coordinated coherent action at the top is critical. However, should not those basic principles be in place day to day and should they not include HR?

As an example of the immense pressures, just consider the comments made about the corporate finance advisers Lazard in 2004. John Gapper in the *Financial Times* wrote about the chairman Michael David-Weill's views about the people at the top: 'Any investment bank is by necessity full of people who are pretty highly strung because the talent needed to win customers is made up in equal parts of confidence in yourself and insecurity.'[2] Gapper went on to observe, 'Investment bankers are very hard to manage – they are as egotistical as actors, with the complication that they measure success in money rather than in applause.' Given the mobility, earnings, ambitions and confidence among talented people in a far wider range of areas than corporate finance, HR needs to be up there at the side of the chairman and the chief executive to influence the outcome.

To deserve this role a good HR person needs business as well as personnel experience, courage, confidence, excellent personal communication skills, humanity and diplomacy. Yet I suspect most HR people did not choose this field because it might, if successful, lead to general management. While few in marketing, finance, legal or operations actually get to the top, it is from these disciplines that to date the most senior managers tend to emerge. Given the importance of people management there is a case for a new breed of senior adviser on strategic as well as operational people matters who matches these traditional sources of senior people in terms of character and ambition.

SHL, the developers, producers and trainers in psychometric tests, conducted some work in the mid-1990s which their then managing director Gill Nyfield kindly shared with me. I asked the question 'How do the psychometrics of HR executives compare with those of other management disciplines?' Gill provided the following characteristics:

HR people are more:	*HR people are less:*
• affiliative	• persuasive
• democratic	• data rational
• caring	• innovative
• behavioural	• organised and structured
• worrying	• critical
	• competitive

The left-hand column contains some admirable attributes, but to carry greater influence with the top team they may need to add some of the qualities on the right.

Do the leaders of the HR community accept these views and what action do they believe is necessary?

Additionally, the historic work priorities of HR have not being conducive to playing a strategic role. The day-to-day administration of recruitment, training, employment legal processes, disputes, industrial tribunals, employee relations and assessment of competitive pay structures all have a high level of administrative requirement. Given most line managers' view that this is what HR is for, it is hard for many to break out into a leading role in organisational development, M&A and the leadership of cultural change. Sometimes I feel that people moving into these big ticket areas can risk having the rug pulled from under them when something goes wrong in the administrative heartland. Wounding verbatims like 'what are you doing on this cultural stuff when you can't even get the payroll right?' indicate the threat.

Bob Baumann, previous chairman of SmithKline Beecham, now GSK, spoke a few years ago to the HR body, Devonshire House, with some powerful advice on these lines.

Your role is to guide strategic and cultural aspects of the business so that it attracts, retains and motivates the people you need to succeed. You cannot do that if you are primarily responsible for the administrative processes of HR.

These issues are well known to the CIPD. They have a difficult path to tread given that the majority of the members and those who attend the major conferences they run, and who read their leading trade publication *People Management*, are not in fact involved day-to-day in the major organisational change issues. They need a trade body that serves and educates them on their day jobs, not something which, while interesting, and sometimes inspiring, does not have any practical benefit for them. In the last year the CIPD has, I think bravely, started to address this issue by commissioning people like the writer Richard Donkin (a regular freelance contributor to the *FT*) to assess the role of HR in change.

Here are some of the main themes of the paper published in June 2004.[3]

Donkin argued that the vital HR agenda in organisational change is often sidelined, leaving HR professionals to pick up the pieces and address the resulting problems after the event. In general, HR people do not lead these programmes, as Bob Baumann said, and have trouble freeing themselves from their day-to-day operational and administrative activities. Donkin states that HR professionals need to move more effectively away from the time they currently spend on administration and pay at least as much attention to the high-level 'change agent role'.

The CIPD is not alone in questioning the HR role and endeavouring to ensure that it is equipped to deal effectively with the many issues we have highlighted. For a start there are thriving subscription bodies like the Corporate Development Council in the US and the Corporate Research Forum in the UK created by the ex-Hewlett-Packard HR executive Mike Haffenden, with Andrew Lambert and me as cofounders. Both of these long-established groups pull no punches when it comes to the need for change in HR. The Corporate Research Forum has worked closely with leading academics in the field, such as Ed Lawler, Jay Conger and the late Sumatra Ghoshal among others. Their high-level contribution needs a powerful, not just a respectful, audience. It is telling that these academics aim their own consulting work at chairmen and CEOs, whereas marketing academics such as Tim Ambler can cut the mustard with Marketing Directors.

Ultimately, we believe that the reputation of HR itself is going to have to change if people of sufficient calibre to eventually achieve a truly senior line job are going to be attracted to spend meaningful time there and be seen as a specialist in the area. HR must be an effective springboard for the top. It is a subject that needs early study to establish the attitudes of those with the requisite character and ability but who have not, so far, considered the HR field. Why have they not done this? What would have to happen within HR to attract them?

One key role within the HR area that is capable of being used as a strategic and political driver of change is the role of employee research. Historically, however, the employee research category is a poor relation within market research overall. Using the Association of Market Survey Organisations' own estimates, only 0.5% of an expenditure of £380 million (a modest £2 million or so) went on HR-related work. Given the fact that there are 27 million people at work in the UK and 40 million adult consumers, we are spending £140 per adult head finding out their opinions on breakfast cereals or motor cars, and only pennies per head on the complex issues associated with their work. If we add the consulting industries HR involvement (which includes considerable qualitative research) we can improve these figures somewhat but we must conclude that many managers believe that they already know their people sufficiently well and do not need further help.

As to what well-judged employee research can do, it is worth mentioning the work done among the 60,000 partners of John Lewis, the UK retail group responsible for John Lewis Department Stores and grocery chain Waitrose. Since the establishment of the John Lewis Partnership in 1929 the group has pioneered the concept of partnership and the involvement of all workers as co-owners. In 2001, they decided to add to their channels of employee listening. They created a regular employee research programme and, with advice from PiB, have created an ongoing process involving a range of branches every month. The response rate has risen from 50% to 87% and the results are now being used in driving many management decisions, at branch, division and partnership level. As the Chairman, Sir Stuart Hampson, recently commented in their in-house magazine[4]:

> I welcome the fact that the Survey has so swiftly become a well established part of our arrangements and that it has opened up such constructive dialogues between managers and their teams to increase the sense of fulfilment, involvement and fun in our business – and, of course, we know that this makes us more commercially successful too.

Overall, we believe that the task of employer brand management will attract a wider range of capable people than HR may have done in the past. You cannot establish a consumer brand without senior management strategic involvement. The same goes for the employer brand. It embodies research, communications, high-level objectives, strategic development and the ability to implement and measure.

Good brand management is not a fad; it is a permanent and enduring approach to good practice in this area. I experienced a graphic example of the power of this approach when working on my first brand, Smith's Crisps. In the early 1960s, Smith's Crisps was an independent company dominated by a managing director called C.J. Scott who had, I recall, married a descendant of the founder, Frank Smith. I say 'dominated' because CJ took all the decisions and was in fact a great client of the W.S. Crawford ad agency in which I was a graduate trainee. We made a notable commercial directed by Dick Lester just after he had directed the Beatles' film 'A Hard Days Night', and our film had the added bonus of featuring Pattie Boyd, George Harrison's girlfriend. How did brand management work at Smith's? The answer was that CJ was quite an effective holder of the role in addition to being managing director. He also had a sales director, a market research manager, sales promotion and advertising managers and a national accounts manager. These were experienced people who were there after long careers with advertising agencies and research companies, but they largely did what they were told. There was little long-term planning and coordination and when, perhaps predictably, Smith's was sold to a classically marketing driven firm, most of those people lost their jobs when a comprehensive marketing approach was adopted.

I finish the chapter with that story because I can see the same thing happening within the world of people management. The individual experts will still have their place but it will be within the context of employer brand management, namely with one approved plan, one set of priorities and rigorous measurement.

The Role of Leadership   5

In the first few years of my consulting in the early 1990s – perhaps when we were assessing the effectiveness of internal communications, doing qualitative employee research or advising on post merger integration – dialogue like this sometimes emerged:

'You'll never get anywhere with this job you know.'

'Why not?'

'Because until the people at the top here are committed to change this project is a waste of time.'

Have you ever felt like that? I can tell you far too many people do and it takes me into this chapter on the importance of senior management's leadership of the development and support for the employer brand. If you are working in a politically sensitive area where roles, responsibility and power are key factors, then you have to get buy-in from the top. And not just buy-in. Any new capital investment like plant and machinery has to get buy-in from the top. Strengthening the employer brand needs more than that, it needs leadership involvement, commitment and courage to overcome the forces of conservatism which can result in an employer brand project being still-born or restricted to tinkering with a different style of recruitment advertising.

We recently did an analysis of the last five years of People in Business's work. You would think that HR were the major buyers but, for many of the reasons we covered in Chapter 4, they are not. Of our revenue over the past five years, 57% has come from working with CEOs and Managing Directors, 28% from HR and 15% from corporate affairs/ internal communications and similar functions.

Employer Brand Management needs active senior leadership because it can mean rocking the status quo, breaking down silos, establishing new roles and relationships, new approaches to measurement and answering difficult questions on what the organisation stands for, and why? What are the behaviours that these values should drive? What is the correct balance of power between the Group and any one of its subsidiaries? The answers to these questions must be teased out from the top and made part of the fabric so that one poor quarter's results or a high-level resignation, or any of the other slings and arrows that regularly beset large organisations, does not succeed in bowling the project over.

I learned the real power of the board in my Colgate days. I remember Reuben Mark (now Chairman) telling brand managers: 'Forget the idea that the brand manager is the managing director of his/her brand. Your job is to know more about your brand in your market than anyone else world wide. Given that knowledge you will be listened to but the power comes from the top.' The brand groups were charged with recommending the plan, covering every aspect of the business, be it formula, packaging, media, creative proposition, distribution, promotion or anything else. However, once that plan was agreed in a formidable budget session with European and Global Management, it became the company's plan not just yours. That was what gave a brand manager the influence and control necessary to ensure delivery through much more senior people with real line authority. It occurs to me that one of HR's issues is that the equivalent of a signed off programme is often lacking so that initiatives have to be constantly sold and resold down the line.

In the majority of successful employer brand programmes we encountered during our research, the CEO played a visible and active role in both development and communication. Of the six work streams making up Reuters' Fast Forward programme, the CEO Tom Glocer chose to take a direct role in leading 'Living Fast', the culture change dimension of the programme that sought to redefine what Reuters would come to mean to its employees (the employer brand). At Nationwide, the CEO, Philip Williamson, made it clear from the beginning of their PRIDE values programme (now in its third year) that these values would play a central role in defining his approach to leading the organisation. As Tom Harvey, Nationwide's head of internal communication, commented: 'While HR have played a significant role in embedding these values, it was clearly Philip's long-term vision and commitment to PRIDE that has encouraged both the slow adopters as well as the early adopters to get on board.'

Sir Terry Leahy has played a similar role at Tesco, as has Michael Bailey at Compass.

Another feature that unites most of these examples is the deep knowledge that each of the CEOs has of the organisation. All of those mentioned above were promoted from within, having managed different parts of the business before becoming CEO. They also share what many have described as the 'common touch'. These are leaders who know what it is like at the 'sharp end' of their business and have not forgotten their roots. As Terry Leahy, who worked his way up through the Tesco ranks from store management, has commented: 'I had a good advantage to grow up in the business. I know how it ticks and was well prepared for my role [as CEO].'[1] Michael Bailey at Compass Group began his career as a chef, and it was clear from our research that his promotion of the Compass employer brand was informed by a deep affinity with his front line staff. Both Tom Glocer of Reuters and Philip Williamson of Nationwide were described as having made important interventions during the process of developing values statements to ensure that they remained simple, engaging and not too over-engineered.

While there are many positive reasons for leaders to take a keen interest in developing and managing the employer brand, there is also a growing negative influence that it can help them to counter. Branding is highly relevant because it shares the same cornerstone as leadership. Flair, style and charisma (like creative advertising) have their place, but the cornerstone of effective leadership is trust. In this respect, many corporate leadership teams appear to be suffering from major subsidence. According to a study by Mercer (*What's Working*) in the UK, only 40% of employees trust their senior management team to communicate with them honestly.[2] Among the UK public at large the picture is even bleaker. In 2003, a poll conducted by MORI for the *FT* found that 80% of people disagreed that 'directors of large companies can be trusted to tell the truth'.[3] This was corroborated by two further surveys conducted the same year. The British Medical Association's annual 'veracity test' found that only a quarter of people trusted business leaders to tell the truth.[4] A further MORI poll conducted among 13 to 18 year olds as part of the *Nestlé Family Monitor* found only 16% of young people believed business leaders could be trusted to tell the truth.[5] This ranked business leaders even lower than government ministers (now that *is* alarming!).

I'm sure I need not dwell on the many reasons why trust appears to be in such short supply. Enron, 'fat cats', financial underperformance, retrenchment on pensions, an increase in redundancies and the resurgence of Union militancy have all played their part in undermining trust in business leadership.

Establishing trust is particularly important for the newly appointed CEO. As soon as a CEO takes up a new position, he or she is on borrowed time. Much like a new brand launch, there is generally a fanfare, but there is also a significant element of 'wait and see'. The first 100 days represent the critical period during which initial expectations are tested, substance is weighed, new relationships are established and change is set in motion. They say that people get judged in an interview situation within the first five minutes. New CEO's may get a little longer to make an impression, but not much longer.

While in some cases the CEOs can be regarded as 'brands' that arrive with high-profile reputations that need to be honed and nurtured, there is much in this perspective that smacks of personal vanity, and it is not the angle that I suggest we focus on. More importantly, new CEOs take on a role at the helm of the corporate brand and it is their potential (and ability) to exert influence over the shape, direction and momentum of this brand that makes up a significant proportion of the 'wait and see'.

Corporate brands are complex entities, with a diverse range of stakeholders. During the first few months, it is sometimes tempting for the CEO to focus most attention on shaping the perceptions of the financial community. The support of investors clearly remains essential, but I would like to focus on another brand relationship which is often just as critical in establishing the trust required to set an organisation on a new course: the employer brand.

With the advent of a new CEO, people within a company generally expect change, and for a few months the CEO has the opportunity to revitalise not only the company's investment rating, but people's perceptions of the company they work for.

So what is there in the brand toolkit that can help the CEO? I would like to suggest six core principles of effective brand management (that we will explore in greater detail in Part II of the book) that could help the CEO through the first 100 days.

1. *Insight* – Great brands are founded on a deep understanding of the relationship between the brand and its audience. How do employees currently perceive the employer brand? Do people have a strong sense of the organisation's purpose and values (both implicit and explicit)? Is there a consistent core of opinion shared by all employees? What behaviours are felt to be most characteristic of the organisation? What currently drives people's commitment and what demoralises people? Why do people choose to join the organisation and why do they leave? (This may be a critical question if the CEO needs to rebuild the management team.) If your employees are asked to describe the kind of organisation they work for, how are they likely to reply?

2. *Focus* – One of the most important roles of branding is to provide a focal point for people's relationship with a product or service. The same holds true for people's relationship with the organisation they work for. The focal point for most effective employer brands tends to be either what the organisation does, or plans to do (the vision, purpose, goals, value-added to customers and consumers) or how they do it (the values, style, culture and personality of the organisation). To make an impact the CEO needs to recognise the current focal point, and if the desire is to drive change, then make the new focal point crystal clear.

3. *Differentiation* – Successful brands constantly need to differentiate themselves. From an employer brand perspective, what is it about the organisation that makes it different from or better than its nearest competitors? If, as a new CEO, you plan to set a new course for the organisation, how will this be different from or better than what has gone before? This may be clear to you, but you need to make it understandable to everyone else.

4. *Benefits* – Effective brand management focuses on benefits not features. This may be a marketing cliché, but this maxim is often overlooked when it comes to internal communication. Simply stated, if you're going to make changes, what's in it for the employees? The answer is seldom more money or greater security, but it could be a greater share in success, competitive strength or wider career opportunities. Don't just assume that employees will read this between the lines.

5. *Continuity* – People lose trust in brands that try to make sudden U-turns. A new CEO needs to understand that for everyone else you are a chapter in an unfolding story, not the beginning of the story. However troubled the present situation, you should recognise the strengths of what has gone before, and stress continuity where you are able. People are far more accepting of change if they can see where it has come from, not just where it is going.

6. *Consistency* – When building trust, consistency is by far the most critical factor. Does what people are hearing have a logical consistency? Even more importantly, is communication consistent with management behaviour, and the concrete changes that employees may be beginning to experience within the organisation? If business leaders followed just one simple brand maxim it would be that *promises need to be matched by clear reasons to believe.*

Let us study a few specific examples of leadership and its impact on the employment experience.

Robert Hiscox is Chairman of the insurance group Hiscox, based in Great St Helens in the City. Originally a family company, now a plc and with Hiscox's own equity now modest, the revenue has grown from £3 million when he took over the management in 1970 to £1 billion in 2004. However, it is not the growth that makes this an interesting story from an employer brand point of view. There is clarity on behaviour; and there is clarity on delegation, often with immense decision-making power given to capable people. Some of the more experienced underwriters can take on up to £25 million of risk without sign-off. There is clarity on who does what at the top, what Hiscox himself does and what his ex-McKinsey Chief Executive Bronek Masojada does. Above all there is an underlying confidence in the leadership that makes it possible for them to admit uncertainty and own up to error. It is an unforgiving place and they do not easily forgive themselves. Finally, that confidence also drives, in my opinion, the humour, humanity and directness in which Hiscox people go about their business together.

Maybe a business with a powerful legacy provides the bedrock of that confidence. I heard the Chief Executive of Timberland, Jeff Schwartz, speak at a Tomorrow's Company event in January 2005, He talked about his grandfather, a Russian immigrant cobbler who arrived in Boston early in the twentieth century and the principles that he felt still drive the continuing success of the modern Timberland business. Now, you may feel that the confidence of men like Hiscox and Schwartz comes from a legacy of financial comfort rather than a legacy of standards, culture, values and behaviour. While there are many cases of family management ruining fine businesses, i.e. clogs to clogs in three generations, I think that there are more powerful drivers than money in the way such leaders as these work. As Professor Schumpeter of Harvard once memorably said, 'Capitalism is not a matter of counting coins. Capitalism is a romance and an adventure', and there has to be an element of that magic in any employer brand. The more a leader feels like that the more powerful their employer brand will be.

I should mention one other great business that is still privately owned. I was the account director on Chanel in my advertising days and worked for Alain Wertheimer when he took over the business, aged 29. The way he has run Chanel reminds me of the quote 'live each day as if it is your last and farm your land as if you are going to live for ever'. In the extraordinarily competitive, ephemeral world of fragrance, beauty and fashion there is, again, confidence, courage and certainty in the basics that has provided a springboard for idea after idea, whether it is the hiring of Karl Lagerfeld in 1986 or the use of Nicole Kidman in Baz Luhrman's Chanel No. 5 commercial in November 2004, reputedly, minute for minute the most expensive film in history. Throughout the fragrances, the cosmetics and the fashion, there is a creative and design surefootedness that instinctively expresses the essence of Chanel. It was there in the Catherine Deneuve advertisements in the 1960s, in the designs and in the behaviours of the executives, many of whom – like Jacques Helleu, who is responsible for Chanel's creative in Paris or Michael Rena the 'consiglione' in New York – have years of service. Yet Wertheimer is not a public leader. He never gives interviews and his legacy will be that Chanel and its employer brand will remain respected at the very top of the market.

I have mentioned three leaders with strong family business roots. Their employer brand leadership stems from a commitment and a longevity of which any business leader should be capable. Someone who has demonstrated both is Sir Martin Sorrell, Chief Executive of WPP. He runs what we believe is one of the most complex employer brands on earth:

84,000 people, over 100 separate companies, built on a philosophy of operational and creative freedom with sharp financial controls. His leadership goes back to 1985, since when the WPP share price has risen from about 27p to around 600p. Over that period he has steadfastly expanded the range of his business and recovered from three crippling share price reverses in 1988, 1991 and 2000. What makes the WPP employer brand so noteworthy is that, on paper at least, his strategy of devolvement and empowerment should place that responsibility into the hands of the leaders of his many businesses, each with a character, identity and positioning of its own. Managing creative businesses can be a nightmare, and that is without asking them to work together. I suspect Sorrell has a very shrewd eye in assessing the correct balance between salaried leadership and unmanageable entrepreneurs. He must have, because I cannot think of any truly damaging breakaway on the lines of Frank Lowe's start-up of Lowe Howard Spink and the industry paper Campaign's headline 'Lowe rips £22 million out of Colletts' (the agency Collett Dickinson and Pearce). Martin Sorrell has judged his leaders just a whisker away from J.K. Galbraith's observation that 'a man works for another when he believes that that man could do better for him than he could do for himself'.[6]

Today, that risk is lessened because of the complexity and international nature of many agency–client relationships. Indeed the WPP employer brand is, almost in spite of itself, being put onto centre stage because of the opportunity for global deals where such clients as Vodafone, Ford, Astra Zeneca, HSBC and Samsung have bought a joined up approach with the responsibility for managing it across the tribes of WPP being the responsibility of WPP itself. Clients may see the good sense in terms of marketing coherence and, no doubt, cost saving, but getting talented independent people, albeit in one group, to work together means that the employer brand of WPP is becoming more important. As Sorrell said in our interview with him for this book, 'Turf, territory and ego are bigger issues at the top of the tribes than at the bottom.' However, the WPP employer brand has some powerful glue. First of all is his realisation that the biggest investment the company makes is in its people. He believes that the $6 billion they spend on people per year can be regarded as an investment rather than a cost, and making the most of this should take much more time and energy than that historically being focused on capital expenditure per year, some $300 million in WPP's case. That thinking has led to a Group-wide incentive scheme, a Marketing Fellowship programme unmatched to date by any of the other major marketing services groups, and demanding expectations of the leaders of his businesses not just in financial terms but in their behaviours. Any marketing services group chief executive who says 'the great managing directors and CEOs make it their business to breakfast, lunch and network the best people in the business all the time' must be worth staying with. Finally, WPP's glue also includes original thought on the marketing services business itself which, for 17 years, has been led by Jeremy Bullmore, a previous chairman of J. Walter Thompson, whose insights, writing and public speaking have long commanded the respect of his industry. All in all, Martin Sorrell's WPP employer brand is a difficult one to leave. It will also be difficult for anyone else to take on the torch of leading it.

For employer brand builders, getting the boss's active enthusiasm and support is critical. The real thing cannot be built without it. Don't start until you have it.

Part II

The 'How To' Guide

Richard Mosley

Brand Fundamentals 6

Until the late twentieth century most people would have only associated the term 'brand' with consumer goods and services. The term is now used far more widely and it is commonplace for the term 'brand' to be used to describe virtually anything carrying a distinct identity, and the reputation, good or bad, associated with that identity. Branding has become the snake oil of modern management. If you believe the brand pundits, branding will cure all ills. It will secure customer loyalty, drive growth, increase profits, induce undying employee commitment to the company's cause, ward off the evil eye of critical investment analysts, reverse national decline, win elections and fill an otherwise drab, mundane and irreligious world with new hope and meaning. Branding has filled every nook and cranny. Self-help gurus have even begun to recommend that people should start thinking of themselves as brands and manage their careers and lives accordingly. The popular media is crammed full of celebrities busily promoting their personal brand image to maintain their place in the light. There is even a 'stock market' where you can track the rise and fall of a celebrity's brand value. People have become justifiably cynical about 'branding', but when you strip away the over-claims, the flim-flam, gloss and spin that often accompany the branding bandwagon, the fundamentals of brand development and management remain extremely valuable.

In the following chapters we will attempt to demonstrate how these fundamentals can be applied to developing and managing the employer brand, but first we would like to define our terms of reference. A vast number of books have been devoted to the general subject of brands and marketing, but even the most common terms, such as 'the brand promise', 'brand proposition' and 'brand positioning', are seldom described in exactly the same way. Before moving on to the task of applying general brand theory to employer brand practice, we will attempt to present a simple guide to the critical components.

FUNCTIONAL BENEFITS

At its simplest, a brand is no more than a badge of identity and promise of performance. It tells you where something (or someone) is from, and it carries an implied guarantee that what has been promised on behalf of the brand will be delivered. Gillette will shave you closer. Persil will wash whiter. Ronseal will do what it says it will do on the back of the can. Even where brands promise something more intangible – style, knowledge, financial security – this tends to be underpinned by some form of tangible functionality. Fashion brands wouldn't survive for long if their clothes fell apart. Information services need to be provided in an accessible format. Insurance companies need to be able to provide you with hard currency if a financial drama turns into a cash crisis.

Employer brands are also founded on a number of basic functional benefits and performance guarantees, such as payment for services rendered, a safe working environment, the provision of the equipment necessary to carry out your roles and responsibilities. These benefits may be implicitly taken for granted, or they may be important elements within your employer brand proposition – top quartile pay, a highly attractive working environment, cutting edge technology.

EMOTIONAL BENEFITS

Brands take tangible form in the functional benefits that they deliver, but they also tend to deliver value in other more subtle and complex ways. I was recently involved in running a series of workshops for Unilever exploring the practical implications of their code of business principles. The section of their code covering consumers included the statement: 'Products and services will be accurately and properly labelled, advertised and communicated.'[1] In the 30 or so workshops that I facilitated for them around Europe, I knew that I was almost guaranteed to raise a laugh if I made the following observation. The advertising for one of their leading deodorant brands strongly implied that it would make me irresistible to women. However, despite my regular use of the product, women didn't appear to be falling over themselves to make my acquaintance. How could this be? Had I missed the small print excluding the less than perfectly attractive? The question to the audience: 'Is this accurate communication?' The strictly 'accurate' answer in terms of 'exact conformity . . . with truth' (*Concise Oxford English Dictionary*) would be 'no'.[2] But, of course, no one regards this as deception. Communication of this kind is seldom so black and white. The promise of irresistibility is acceptable in this case, because it is only implied not stated, and it comes wrapped in irony. The intended result is that not only will people believe the functional promise that this brand will be an efficacious deodorant, but that the brand will be associated (on a more emotive level) with the tongue-in-cheek self-confidence and sexual appeal to which the target audience aspires. In short, it will promote a relevant and attractive emotional benefit that serves to 'position' the more functional benefits of the product in the mind of the consumer. In a similar fashion, most brands have shifted their main focus away from what the brand does (easy to copy) to how it will make you feel (easier to differentiate).

Emotional engagement is currently a hot topic in the world of work, and the psychological benefits associated with employer brands are just as important as they are to branded products and services. It has long been recognised that there is more to motivation than pay, incentives or coercion, the 'kick in the ass' approach to motivation debunked long ago by Herzberg.[3] People's emotional attachment to their employer tends to be driven by the value they derive from the total work experience, including the inherent satisfaction they derive from the tasks they perform, the extent to which they feel valued by their colleagues, and their belief in the quality, purpose and values of the organisation they represent. How this 'psychological contract' is communicated and delivered forms an essential counterpart to the more tangible functional 'terms and conditions' incorporated in the formal employment contract.

HIGHER ORDER BENEFITS, BRAND VALUES AND DNA

As brands are extended across a range of different products and services the promises made on their behalf tend to migrate to higher ground. Charles Revlon famously claimed that while other companies sold cosmetics, Revlon sold hope. Similarly, the deodorant Lynx had shifted the core focus for the brand away from the specific functionality of deodorising towards male attractiveness. These higher order benefits – confidence, freedom, well-being, refreshment – are often described in terms of brand values or in a more distilled form, the DNA or essence of the brand. They tend to be the primary focus of brand communication and image-building, with the more specific functional performance of individual products and services providing the tangible 'reasons to believe'.

When these image associations are strong they can also enhance people's physical experience of the branded product. In tests, people typically give identical products higher performance scores when they are branded than when they are unbranded. People's headaches clear up faster when they know the brand name. Likewise, Coca-Cola tastes more refreshing when people know it is Coca-Cola.

The ground-breaking study *Built to Last*, written by Collins and Porras in 1995, prompted a host of business leaders to set off in search of their corporation's inner purpose and values.[4] These core attributes were couched in very similar terms to the higher order values and benefits used to describe product and service brands, but these two streams have generally failed to come together in a satisfactory union. In a holding company one can understand the need to define a number of high-level principles within which the total family of companies should operate, but when the brand defines both the organisation and its products and services, is there really room for two competing sets of values – one set for the organisation, the other for the services it advertises externally. It reminds me of the Groucho Marx line: 'I have principles, and if you don't like them I have others.' The purpose of the employer brand proposition is not to invent a further set of values, but to help to ensure that the purpose and value statements that currently exist are translated into something relevant and meaningful to employees, and made consistent with the values the organisation wishes to project externally.

BRAND PERSONALITY

While this range of functional, emotional and higher order benefits describes what the brand can do for you, the style, tone and range of references used to communicate these benefits represent a further dimension of branding, generally referred to as 'brand personality'. Brand personality is a useful metaphor since, like brands, we tend to be attracted to people who display both individuality and reasonable predictability over time. In forming a relationship, we like to know where we stand with people. The same is true of brands. Just as personality defines the patterns we seek (and come to expect) in our relationships with people, brand personality helps us to familiarise and identify (or not) with different choices of brand. The personality of some brands is largely defined and represented by their founder. The personality traits of Virgin – enterprising, irreverent, and fun – are largely felt to be personified by Richard Branson. Others pay large sums of money to be endorsed by celebrities whose personalities they hope will become closely associated with the brand. A classic example of this is Nike's association with the basketball superstar Michael Jordan. A more recent example is Accenture's association with Tiger Woods. The personality of most brands, however, is built up in a more piecemeal fashion over time. The personality of brands that have been around for many years – Pepsi, Guinness, Marlboro, Shell – tend to derived from a more complex mix of long-term heritage, old advertising campaigns, and most recent marketing activity. Where these brands have been managed well over time (which applies to most of the long-term survivors) there always appears to be that underlying core of consistency and familiarity you would expect of an old friend.

'Authenticity' is a key word in the brand lexicon. The brand personality of packaged products generally comes down to carefully constructed communication. The personality of a service brand is far more difficult to fabricate and control, since it tends to be deeply rooted in the culture of the organisation and the character and behaviour of the many different types of people the organisation relies on to deliver its service to the customer. The employer brand probably represents the ultimate test in authenticity, since it is virtually impossible to misrepresent the culture and personality of an organisation to those people who experience it at first hand 40–60 hours a week. Defining the employer brand personality, therefore, comes down to both an insightful reading of the current culture, and people's shared (and reasonably realistic) aspirations.

BRAND POSITIONING AND DIFFERENTIATION

The benefits, values and personality traits described above can only mean something if they are defined in relation to a target audience that values what is being offered. Every brand is surrounded by alternatives competing for their share of attention, interest and loyalty. Brands need to be focused to compete effectively in this crowded space, and brand positioning represents the art and science of targeting the right audiences with the most compelling benefits and brand messages.

To be compelling most brands need to emphasise what makes them different and better at fulfilling the needs of this target group. This is a tricky business since, as we have discussed, most functional benefits are soon copied. This means that in addition to delivering constant improvements to ensure that the functional performance of the product or service remains competitive, brands also need to develop and defend a position in the marketplace that they can uniquely own. This is where the brand image and personality plays a critical role in both anchoring the brand (what stays the same as the functionality changes), and differentiating the brand in the mind of the consumer. Returning to the deodorant market, Lynx, Sure and Dove deodorants come in almost identical formats, and function equally effectively. However, Lynx is targeted at young men and focuses on attractiveness, Dove is targeted at women and focuses on being gentler on the skin, and the more unisex Sure focuses on keeping you dry even in the sweatiest circumstances.

This distillation of the most relevant, differentiating and compelling brand descriptors for a given target group is generally referred to as a brand proposition. You will note the use of 'a' not 'the' brand proposition. This is because there may be both a 'core' brand proposition relevant to all audiences and a range of sub-propositions defining the key benefit and message for more specific subgroups of the audience (including employees).

New brands tend to be positioned relatively narrowly in terms of both target audience and benefit. As brands become more mature and successful they tend to extend their 'footprint' by offering different benefits to the same target group, or the same benefits to different target groups. Gillette's extension into female razors (with the sub-brand Venus) from its strongly held position in premium priced, high-performance, disposable razors for men, is a classic example of the second of these approaches. The user group (gender, age, etc.) is only one of many potential ways to define and segment a market. You can also define your market position by product type (disposable vs electric); price (premium Gillette vs bargain Bic); occasion (home vs away); distribution channel (supermarket vs vending machine). Positioning offers endlessly new permutations both for brand leaders to extend their dominance and challenger brands to get a foothold.

The art of brand positioning is highly relevant to the employer brand proposition in two very important respects. The first and most obvious of these is that employees represent an important target group for the brand with distinctly different needs and aspirations from customers and consumers. For the brand to be relevant and motivating to employees it needs to be positioned to meet these needs and aspirations. It is also valuable to consider whether the proposition is clearly differentiated. What can the organisation offer its potential candidates and current employees that make it better or different from the other alternatives open to them? Once this is accepted as making good sense, the next logical step is to recognise that current employees and potential candidates for employment are likely to be as diverse (if not more diverse) than the company's customer base. In the war for talent, and the competition for commitment, targeting the right audiences with the right brand messages and benefits is as critical for the employer brand as for the customer brand.

BRAND HIERARCHY

You will note the introduction of sub-branding in the above example. The concept of brand hierarchy is used to define the relationships within a family of brands. At the product level Venus is unique in some respects (defining a product range designed for women) while benefiting from (and reinforcing) some of the associations shared across the total Gillette range (particularly its 'cutting edge' credentials in shaving). As with brand positioning, getting the brand hierarchy right involves a careful balancing act. In this case between maintaining the focus and credentials of the 'parent brand', and the more tailored positioning of the sub-brand. Gillette probably chose to sub-brand Venus because 'Gillette for women' may have felt too masculine. Nevertheless, Gillette's endorsement of Venus gave it performance credentials it may have lacked going alone.

This balancing act becomes extremely relevant in the employer brand context when you are trying to manage the relationship between a 'parent' corporate brand (e.g. Whitbread) and its separately branded operating companies (e.g. Costa Coffee, Lloyd Leisure and Marriot hotels). To what extent should employees identify with the corporate brand? What degree of influence should the corporate owner try to exert over the employment experience of its company portfolio? These are some of the key employer brand hierarchy questions that we will address in Chapter 9.

BRAND VISION AND BRAND REALITY

It is important for those tasked with developing and managing brands to spend quality time and effort defining the key components of the brand. This definition is typically enshrined in an idealised model (the brand key, diamond, pyramid, etc.). This model brand typically provides the starting point for the brand strategy, with an emphasis on finding the most effective way of getting its message across to the target audience. The inherent danger in this approach is forgetting that the model you have defined is a vision of the brand as you would like people to see it, not the brand reality. The real brand lives not in the model, but in people's everyday experience of the brand and the rather more untidy cluster of perceptions and associations that they carry around in their heads. The reason this is important is that if brand communication strays too far from the perceived reality of the brand it can feel phoney or, worse, set up expectations that fail to be delivered. People are understandably cynical about brands that promise much, but fail to live up to expectations, brands that are all show and no substance. These are the brands that give branding a bad name. To counter this overemphasis on the idealised brand many brand-led companies like Unilever insist on two definitions of the brand, the first describing the brand as it is currently perceived and experienced, warts and all (the brand reality), and the second describing how the company would like it to be perceived and experienced (the brand vision). To get to where you want to get to it helps to be very clear about where you currently are.

This gap between vision and reality is extremely pertinent to employer brands. Corporate policy and value statements appear particularly prone to aspirational over-claim. It is not only the expensive gloss of the paper that makes employees feel that corporate literature is out of touch. It is also the tendency of corporate communication to gloss over the everyday realities of the employment experience in their assertion of what the company claims to stand for or offer its employees.

BRAND MANAGEMENT AND DEVELOPMENT

The task of most brand managers who inherit an existing brand is to close the gap between the current brand reality and the brand vision. This requires them to steer a course between what may initially appear to be two contradictory goals. The first goal is to maintain the clarity, consistency and continuity of the brand. The second goal is to introduce changes that will help to develop, stretch and refresh the brand. Striking the right balance between these two tasks is a constant challenge. Change too much and the brand will lose focus; change too little and the brand will lose relevance.

Brand Consistency and Continuity

At the most fundamental level brands need to present a clear and consistent visual identity. Brands are usually governed by strict identity guidelines that determine how the brand logo should appear, which colours and fonts should be used in association with the brand and even the type of imagery that should be used. One of the basic roles of brand management is to ensure that these guidelines are being followed. Given the tendency of people within large and relatively disparate organisations to 'do their own thing', corporate brand identity generally requires constant policing to keep it on track.

The second and more difficult task is to ensure that everything the company communicates about the brand remains clear and consistent. There is now a bewilderingly wide range of potential channels for brand communication. Ensuring that your packaging, advertising, direct mail, point of sale materials, sponsorships and other assorted media combine to reinforce the same key brand messages and associations, represents a huge challenge to brand managers, particularly when the 'creative' work for these channels is handled by a number of different agencies. Ensuring a strong degree of continuity over time is also a major challenge when there is constant temptation to try something new. Many brands have fallen by the wayside having switched and changed tack numerous times to attract short-term attention, while some of the most successful have been relentlessly consistent over time in reinforcing the same core brand proposition. The premium lager Stella Artois is a classic example of a brand that has grown year on year for the last decade by sticking consistently to the same "reassuringly expensive" message.

While less of an issue for packaged goods, the third and most difficult task for service brands is to deliver a brand experience that consistently delivers on the underlying proposition. While there are typically a number of functional components within a service offering that can give your brand an edge, the most important factor in shaping perceptions of a service brand tends to be your people. This represents a step change in managing the brand experience which many service companies are still struggling to come to terms. It also represents a critical issue in employer brand management. As Dr Graeme Martin and Professor Phillip Beaumont[5] state in their excellent review of the relationship between branding and people management: 'It is widely recognised that satisfaction with service brands is intimately related to the expected and perceived behaviour of employees, which is often the most difficult factor to control in the marketing mix. However, this [marketing] literature is rooted in the belief that communications are the main source and solution for all organisational problems. It tends to restrict the role of HR to communicating brand values, rather than being the source of such values and the driver of key aspects of strategy.'

In turning our attention to managing employee's perceptions and experience of the employer brand it is surprising how many organisations seem to disregard even the most basic rules of external brand management. Even when the presentation of the main corporate logo is rigorously policed it is common within many organisations to find hundreds of internal sub-identities promoting different regions, divisions, departments, internal channels, change programmes and policy initiatives. The lack of basic brand discipline becomes equally evident when you consider internal communication. It is fairly typical for multiple sources within an organisation to be pumping out communication with little regard to a common agenda, and the roll-call of corporate campaigns seldom displays any continuity over time. The latest big message is always the most important, until it is superseded and contradicted by the next big message. Putting all of these sub-identities and campaign initiatives on one page (if they will fit) is an exercise that soon reveals why employees often feel overburdened and confused by organisational complexity. As Linda Gratton[6] so eloquently puts it:

> In the rush to change there is an overwhelming desire to start again, to deny the past, to continuously look for the new formulae – consistency and continuity are destroyed. Employees are the victims of a stream of new initiatives and management despair when the quick fix fails to materialize.

If employees were treated with the same care and respect as customers, this kind of inconsistency and confusion would never be tolerated.

Brand Development

While a strong degree of consistency and continuity are imperative for maintaining the integrity and credibility of a brand, brands can never afford to stand still. People's needs, aspirations and tastes change over time. Competing brands will forever be striving to offer new and better alternatives. Against this evolving background brand managers constantly need to refresh the way in which the brand is communicated and delivered. Products and services need to be constantly improved and upgraded. Think of the way in which the VW Golf has evolved over time, or Microsoft Windows. Brand communication requires constant creative attention to find new ways of dramatising brand messages. Brand managers also need to explore new avenues for stretching and growing the brand by extending the product range, targeting new audiences or taking the brand into new geographical territory. Brands are either growing or dying. There is no middle ground.

One of the most difficult issues facing internal brand programmes is the question of maintaining momentum. From our perspective this is because the agenda for ongoing development tends to be weak. All the focus tends to be on the launch, getting the message across, making an impact, after which the agenda switches to bedding in and maintenance. Ongoing brand management needs to be about more than policing. Employees needs and aspirations also change. To grow and flourish, employer brands need constant renewal and refreshment.

Brand management has been successfully applied to building brand reputation and winning the commitment and loyalty of customers for over 70 years. As many companies are beginning to realise, the 'joined-up' discipline of brand management can equally be applied to attracting, retaining and engaging your most valued employees (from your top 'strategic' talent to your frontline 'brand ambassadors'). As we hope to demonstrate, there is far more to employer branding than 'sexing up' your recruitment materials or running a 'living the brand' internal communications campaign. The following chapters provide a practical step-by-step guide to developing and implementing an employer brand strategy that not only delivers on your immediate business objectives, but also helps to ensure that your brand is built to last.

SUMMARY

1. While the use of branding for superficial image manipulation has resulted in a degree of cynicism, the fundamental disciplines of brand management remain extremely valuable.
2. Strong brands offer clearly defined functional and emotional benefits.
3. They are characterised by enduring values and personality traits.
4. They are clearly positioned in the minds of their target audiences and differentiated from their competitors.
5. The parent and subsidiary relationships within the brand family are clearly defined and mutually supportive.
6. They retain a solid core of consistency while constantly developing fresh avenues for expressing and delivering value.

The Business Case 7

The first question you'll need to address before developing an employer brand plan is: How can a stronger employer brand help the organisation to achieve its objectives? This chapter will attempt to provide some general answers to this question relating to goals that are common to most organisations. These include lowering costs, increasing customer satisfaction and, ultimately, delivering higher than average return on investment and profitability. We will also try to provide some more specific answers relating to organisational life stages and 'rites of passage'.

THE MAJOR BENEFITS OF EMPLOYER BRANDING

The three major benefits of employer branding identified in research conducted by Hewitt Associates,[1] The Conference Board[2] and The Economist[3] are generally cited as being enhanced recruitment, retention and employee engagement/commitment. Similar studies that have explored the benefits of being an 'employer of choice' (suggesting a strong employer brand reality, though not necessarily the conscious or explicit application of employer brand management) cite very similar benefits. While these improvements do not necessarily represent business benefits by and of themselves, there is a broad range of further evidence to suggest that these three factors can contribute significantly to overall business performance.

Lower Costs

While the primary role of brands is generally to add value, strong employer brands can also help to reduce costs. A North American study conducted by Towers Perrin in 2003, involving 35 000 employees in the

USA and 4500 in Canada, revealed a clear correlation between levels of employee engagement and cost of goods sold.[4] The most significant area in which costs can be reduced is in recruitment. Setting aside the cost of growing the organisation, the cost of replacing employees – even to remain the same size – represents a significant burden in most industry sectors. In their study *United States at Work 2000*, human capital consultants, AON, estimated that replacing an employee costs half of his or her annual salary.[5] US Conference Board estimates have been very similar for entry level employees; however, for middle managers they estimated the level as being closer to one and a half times annual salary and for senior management level, two and a half times.[6] If your staff turnover is lower than that of your competitors it will provide you with an obvious advantage in terms of your cost base, and strong employer brands tend to enjoy higher levels of employee retention. The Nationwide Building Society, which came top of the *Sunday Times* list of *Best Big Companies to Work For* in 2005, has a turnover rate of 9% against an industry average of 15%. An internal source estimated that this equated to a cost benefit of approximately £1.5 million per percentage point per annum, based on an average cost of £8500 for recruiting and inducting each new member of staff. The relationship between strong employer brands and high levels of retention was further confirmed by a US study conducted by Hewitt Associates and Vanderbilt University.[7] This research found that the average employee turnover rate of the Fortune *100 Best Companies to Work for in America* was 12.6% compared to the general average of 26% resulting in significantly reduced recruitment costs.

Sickness absence is also a major cost burden to many organisations. In 2000 the UK's Industrial Society estimated that sickness absence cost the country £13 billion a year, including both the direct cost of sick pay and the more indirect costs involved in lost production, disruption, reduced efficiency and lost opportunity.[8] In 2003, a UK retail bank study involving 20000 employees conducted by the leading employee research firm ISR, discovered that bank branches with above-average employee attitude and engagement scores experienced a 14% lower level of absenteeism than those that were below average.[9] The Conference Board estimates a loss of $165 per missed workday per employee in the USA and recent research undertaken by TNS identified that disengaged employees take an average of 11 days more sick time per year.[10]

While recruitment, retention and sickness absence represent some of the most clear-cut areas in which costs can be saved, there is also evidence to suggest that high levels of organisational engagement can help to reduce costs across a number of other less obvious areas. In their 2003 report, *Understanding the People and Performance Link*, the UK's Work and Employment Research Centre studied 12 leading UK organisations over two years.[11] Their findings from a detailed study of Tesco stores were particularly revealing in their demonstration that higher levels of employee engagement were not only linked to higher overall performance, but also to important operational efficiency factors such as wastage (known loss) and shrinkage (unknown loss through theft and stock errors).

Customer Satisfaction

The rallying cry for many service organisations over the last decade has been 'living the brand'. This follows a recognition that differentiation in the marketplace is generally reliant on the overall quality of the service experience, and this experience is heavily reliant on the way in which employees behave towards customers. While employees' understanding of the customer brand proposition is clearly important, it is generally accepted that the motivation to truly 'live the brand' requires a more general commitment to (and from) the organisation. Most research into the employee's role in delivering customer satisfaction has therefore focused on the broader concept of employee engagement and commitment (to the employer brand).

The most quoted case study in this area is probably the US retailer, Sears Roebuck. In the late 1990s Sears set out to explore the link between three key questions:

- Is Sears a compelling place to work for employees? (employer brand perspective).
- Is Sears a compelling place to shop for customers? (customer brand perspective).
- Is Sears a compelling place for investors? (financial brand perspective).

What Sears discovered from its survey data from 800 stores was that employee satisfaction accounted for between 60% and 80% of customer satisfaction, and that a 5 unit increase in employee satisfaction correlated with a 1.3 unit increase in customer satisfaction, which in turn delivered a 0.5% increase in revenue. This was one of a number of studies on which Heskett et al. reported in their excellent book *The Service Profit Chain*.[12]

The link between employee engagement and customer satisfaction has since been corroborated by a number of further major studies. The Institute for Employment Studies' UK report *From People to Profits*,[13] involving research with 65000 employees across 100 stores of a major British retailer, demonstrated a strong correlation between employee commitment, customer satisfaction (0.23) and sales (0.26). The Gallup Organisation's Q12 Workplace Survey applied to a group of US retail companies in the late 1990s found that the top quartile stores for employee satisfaction were associated with 39% above-average customer satisfaction scores.[14] ISR's retail bank syndicate study (2003) identified that those branches with upper quartile engagement levels were associated with 20% higher levels of 'extremely satisfied' customers than those in the lowest quartile.[9] Standard Chartered Bank's study of their own employee engagement and performance links similarly demonstrated that retail branches with highly engaged employees were 1.7 times more likely to achieve above-average customer satisfaction ratings.[15]

While the majority of these studies have focused on retail organisations, there is also evidence to suggest that similar correlations between employee engagement and customer satisfaction can also be demonstrated in other service sectors. The business to business, communications technology company Nortel Networks claims to have identified conclusive evidence from its own research of a clear link between employee engagement and customer satisfaction.[16] Similarly, Sun Microsystems has claimed to have found a strong link between 'the likelihood of employees to recommend Sun as a place to work and the likelihood that customers will recommend Sun as a place to do business'.[16]

Financial Results

While reducing costs and increasing customer satisfaction provide a strong business rationale for focusing greater attention on the employer brand, the case ultimately rests on demonstrating a clear link between the strength of the employer brand, high levels of employee engagement and financial performance.

Many of the retail studies quoted above have put a figure on the financial implications of higher employee engagement. The Sears study concluded that a 4% increase in employee satisfaction translated into more than $200 million in additional revenue. The IES *From People to Profits* study of a UK retailer demonstrated that an increase of one point in employee commitment to the organisation (on a five-point scale) delivered a 9% increase in sales per store, worth £200 000.[13] In addition to reducing the costs associated with absenteeism and increasing general levels of customer satisfaction, ISR's retail bank study also identified that a 10% improvement in employee attitudes/engagement to the organisation would add 2.5% to the value of sales in the branch network per year.[9] Standard Chartered Bank's study[15] found that retail branches with highly engaged employees were associated with greater revenue growth (+6%) and greater profit margin growth (+100%).

These positive correlations between employee engagement and positive financial results are not limited to the retail sector. The most significant study in this area has probably been ISR's three-year global study (1999–2001) involving 360 000 employees from 41 companies across a range of industry sectors.[17] The results demonstrated a strong correlation between levels of employee commitment to the organisation and changes in both operating margins and net profit margins. On average, those companies with high levels of employee commitment increased their operating margins by 3.74% over the three-year period, compared to a decline of 2.01% among those with low commitment. Likewise, high-commitment companies increased their profit margins by an average of 2.06% over the period compared with a 1.38% decline among low-commitment companies.

In Watson Wyatt's *Work USA* study[18] involving research with 12 750 workers across a range of different industry sectors, they demonstrated that the three-year total return to shareholders was 36% higher in organisations with high-employee commitment (112%) compared with low-employee commitment (76%).

A study conducted by the Frank Russell Company demonstrated that between 1998 and 2002 those organisations featured in the UK *Sunday Times* list of *100 Best Companies to Work For* delivered a compounded annual return of 12.1% compared with a 5.8% overall decline in the FTSE ALL Share index.[19] Likewise, those organisations featured in the Fortune *100 Best Companies to Work For in America* delivered a return of 9.86% compared with a marginal decline in the S&P 500 as a whole over a similar period.

Summary

There is significant evidence to suggest that a strong employer brand, associated with higher than average levels of employee engagement, will help you to reduce costs, improve customer satisfaction, and ultimately contribute to better financial results. These are general business benefits that are relevant to all organisations. There are also a number of further potential benefits relating to specific life stages and 'rites of passage' for the organisation.

LIFE CYCLE BENEFITS

Young, Fast Growing Companies: Attracting 'The Right Stuff'

For relatively new companies the primary benefit of having a clear employer brand proposition is the role it can play in helping to attract and retain good-quality candidates. If the company has ambitious growth plans, but a low profile, it is often a strain to find the right people to match the ambition and qualities of the founders, particularly the reserves of energy and fortitude required to grow from a small to medium-sized enterprise. In most fast-growing entrepreneurial businesses the employer brand tends to develop relatively organically, and in many cases the employer brand is a direct extension of the founder's personality. The Body Shop original employer brand was probably 90% Anita Roddick; Richer Sounds, 90% Julian Richer; and Carphone Warehouse, 90% Charles Dunston. Nevertheless, a well-articulated employer brand proposition can help to clarify the scope of the company's ambition, the type of people it is looking for to help to develop the business, and the characteristics that make it both distinctive and likely to succeed. Rather than residing in formal values statements, these characteristics are often quite quirky cultural signifiers. The implicit character of the Added Value Group, a five-year old, fast-growing marketing agency that Richard Mosley joined in 1995, was summed up in the shared language of 'the Christmas party test' (not as bad as it sounds), 'radiators' (upbeat personality types) and the Generator (an approach to brainstorming ideas that neared the status of religious ritual). Alongside the character of the two founding partners, these reference points were important in making the agency feel unique and reinforced a strong sense of shared identity and belonging. Allister Jones, the Communications Director of Carphone Warehouse, described similarly distinctive forms of language and behaviour that typified the early days of one of the UK's most successful entrepreneurial companies of the last decade.

Coming of Age: Capturing the Organisational Spirit

In Malcolm Gladwell's excellent book, *The Tipping Point*, he talks about the significance to an organisation of growing beyond 150 employees.[20] He makes the point that from hunter-gatherer societies and agricultural colonies to military organisations, this number represents a natural tipping point for communities. Beyond this point, the personal familiarity, peer pressure and informally shared ethos that binds the group together begins to break down, and more formal hierarchies, rules and regulations tend to be required to maintain group order and solidarity. Whether or not 150 represents the natural point of transition, the business benefit of developing an employer brand proposition as an organisation grows from feeling small and personal to large and impersonal is to help to identify and retain something of the spirit that drove the early success of the organisation and made it feel 'special' to its employees.

Going International: Translating the Employer Brand into New Contexts

The benefit of capturing the spirit and essence of the organisation in some form of employer brand proposition becomes even more important when a company expands internationally. One of the reasons that Tesco probably put such great emphasis on making its core values explicit in the mid 1990s was that it was beginning to step up the process of international expansion that began in Hungary in 1994, and 10 years later accounted for over 40% of the retailer's floor space. It soon became clear to Tesco that in building an international brand presence, exporting the Tesco values was as important as transferring the company's operational and financial practices. When first setting up shop in a different country, employees seldom have prior experience of the organisation as a customer, and expectations of management, employment and customer service can vary significantly from what may be taken for granted in the home country. For this reason, Tesco sends its very best managers to embody the Tesco ethos in new countries rather than relying on the operating manual. As David Reid, Tesco's deputy chairman, recently put it: 'We send our best people abroad, people who are good with people, and who can translate Tesco values into the local market.'[21]

Merger and Acquisition: Forging a Shared Sense of Identity and Purpose

Mergers and acquisitions involve a distinct set of new challenges for organisations in addition to those involved in organic growth. The overriding business goal in most M&As is to reduce the shared cost base and add greater value through leveraging the complementary strengths of each organisation. The first of these goals tends to be far more straightforward than the second. Reducing head-count generally requires a more clear-cut intervention than getting different groups of people to work together to generate new sources of value. The business benefit of an employer brand strategy in this context is to help to define and communicate this shared platform for future growth and prosperity.

M&As mark a significant 'moment of truth' for employer brands. In attempting to forge a common sense of purpose and identity from two previously separate employer brands, the senior management team has to address a number of difficult questions.

1. How different are the existing employer brands from each other in terms of the implicit (cultural) and explicit (contractual) relationship with employees?
2. What are the respective advantages and disadvantages of maintaining each employer brand vs subsuming one within the other, or creating a new brand?
3. To what extent should the culture and values of the organisations be actively hybridised to create something stronger?

The answer to these questions will determine whether the primary employer brand task is: creating a common core (e.g. Compass); advocacy and assimilation (e.g. Vodafone subsuming numerous companies across

Europe to create a commonly branded network); or reinvention (e.g. the creation of Diageo from Guinness, United Distillers and IDV).

Corporate Reinvention: Refreshing the Self-Image

There comes a time in the life of any organisation when it feels the need to reinvent itself, and this transition is often accompanied by a new corporate identity. The business case for employer brand development in this context is the need to ensure that the employee experience and sense of renewal matches up to the more superficial revitalisation of the visual identity. New corporate identities always seem to meet the same question: Has the organisation really changed, or is it just image manipulation? Given the raised expectations and carping cynicism that accompany most identity changes, there is a significant need to demonstrate that the change is more than skin deep. From an employer brand perspective, most employees will realise that the organisation is unlikely to change overnight with the advent of new signage, but they will expect to be clear about the new direction, refreshed sense of purpose and value that underpin the transformation in identity. Employees are also likely to expect some substantive changes in addition to the new look. Consider, for example, the internal expectations (and scope for cynicism) raised by BP's Helios mark and associated mission to propel the company 'beyond petroleum'.

To a greater or lesser extent (depending on the frequency of change and the profile of the new incumbent) similar expectations tend to greet the arrival of a new CEO. With the advent of a new CEO people within a company generally expect change, and for a few months the CEO has the opportunity to revitalise not only their investment rating, but people's perceptions of the company they work for (the employer brand).

Revitalising the Customer Brand Proposition: Living the Brand

In many cases, but not always, corporate revitalisation is accompanied by a new service promise to customers. Classic brand repositionings of this kind include the 1960s Avis campaign *'We're number two, we try harder'*, the 1970s TSB campaign *'The bank that likes to say yes'*, Midland Bank's *'The listening bank'* and the 1990s Fedex campaign *'Whatever it takes'*. The primary business need in this case is to ensure that employees perform appropriately to meet raised customer expectations and deliver on the brand promise. What if your employees don't try hard enough? Feel obliged to say no? Aren't very good listeners? Then you have a problem. The role of the employer brand in ensuring that employees both understand and commit to the new service promise is to identify how the organisation's treatment of employees can model the kind of brand experience they are expected to deliver to customers. Employees are unlikely to 'live the brand' unless they experience it for themselves, and if employees fail to deliver on the brand promise, the investment in marketing the new message is likely to be counterproductive.

Burning Platform: Re-instilling Fresh Belife

If you have suffered a major blow to profitability due to a shift in market conditions or, worse, your corporate reputation has suffered a nosedive because of misdemeanours at the top of the organisation, it is likely that your employer brand reputation will require as much remedial attention as your financial balance sheet. The Reuters case study in Appendix 1 provides a classic example of how redefining and relaunching employer brand values can help to re-instill a strong sense of self-belief in employees and hasten the return to financial growth.

Functional Benefits

This chapter has so far covered the potential benefits of strengthening the employer brand to the overall business. You may also wish to take a more functional perspective. What's in it for the HR function? Marketing function? Communications function? We believe that it is worth addressing each of these in turn, as demonstrating the benefit of employer branding to each of these key functions can have a major impact on how successful the organisation is in constructing a truly 'joined up' employer brand strategy.

Benefits to the HR Function

In Chapter 4 we addressed the need for change within HR, particularly the recognised need to adopt a more strategic perspective. We believe the employer brand approach can help in making this transition by addressing two of the central paradoxes at the heart of strategic HR management. As Dave Ulrich pointed out in his influential call to action, *Human Resource Champions*, the first of these challenges is HR's role as both strategic partner to the business and employee champion.[22] As he states: 'Resolving this conflict requires that all parties – HR, management and employees – recognise that HR professionals can both represent employees and implement management agendas.' In a similar way the tools of brand management are designed to address this balancing act by helping to define and mediate between the value of the brand to customers and to the business. It's generally in the customer's interest to demand more for less. It's generally in the business's interest to offer less for more. If this sounds familiar in the context of employee pay negotiations, we believe there is a distinct benefit in extending this conscious and explicit balancing act to the broader relationship (the 'psychological contract') between the employee and the organisation.

The second paradox is the requirement for HR to be both agents of change and guardians of stability. As Ulrich points out: 'Businesses must balance the past and the future . . . the benefits of free agency and control . . . efficiency and innovation.' As we stated in the previous chapter, this second balancing act is also a central feature of effective brand management, and we believe that the well-honed tools associated with this discipline can be of great benefit to the HR profession in addressing this complex and highly demanding challenge.

A further major benefit of adopting the employer brand approach is the scope it provides for more seamless integration with the 'external' business agenda. For example, the marketing and HR functions often fail to agree because they tend to use different language and models to describe very similar objectives. Adopting a 'joined-up' model of internal and external brand relationship management can help to clarify and resolve many of these apparent conflicts and ensure that the internal and external agendas can be brought into closer alignment.

Benefits to the Internal Communications Function

Employees seldom express much satisfaction with the quality of internal communication within their organisation. They generally feel overloaded with apparently irrelevant and inconsistent information from too many different sources. This is seldom the direct fault of the communications function which generally appreciates the need for more joined-up communications planning. It tends to result from the failure of senior line managers (and colleagues from other functions) to consider either the bigger strategic picture or the perspective of the audience. The principal benefit of taking an employer brand approach is the way in which it encourages senior line managers to view employee communication in a more similar light to customer communication. It reinforces the strategic role of internal communication in shaping how people perceive the organisation and its leadership. Employees seldom trust a management team that continues to send them inconsistent messages. It encourages managers to think in terms of target audiences, headline messages, benefit-led persuasion and audience response, rather than just 'getting the communication out'. The end benefit to employees should be greater clarity and less information overload, and to the communications function an enhanced effect on engagement, performance and professional respect from their peers.

Benefits to the Marketing Function

One of the most common complaints we hear from marketing people within service businesses is that their sphere of influence is seldom allowed to extend beyond brand communication. The employer brand perspective can provide an effective platform for transforming this notion of brand as communication to something more deeply rooted in the structure, process and behaviour of the organisation. It can help to provide a more effective bridge between marketing and HR, and, just as essentially, between marketing and the leadership agenda for organisational change. As Tim Ambler puts it in his book *Marketing and the Bottom Line*:[23]

> The similarities and market-driving potential of employee-based brand equity should encourage HR and marketing to swap notes . . . Just as the provision of metrics for the Exec presents an opportunity to rethink the relationship between marketing and finance functions, so employer brand equity provides a challenge bridging marketing and HR skills and information.

Finally, we believe that employer brand management can help to deliver greater impact and credibility to internal marketing programmes that seek to promote understanding of the brand, and the essential role that employees play in delivering a consistent brand experience. As Pringle and Gordon commented in *Brand Manners*[24]:

> All the good work on brand positioning, marketing and communication can easily be undone by a poor interaction between a customer and a brand representative . . . How often has a customer-employee 'moment of truth' turned into a relationship killer, rather than a loyalty builder?

Once employees recognise the brand in their own experience of work, they are far more likely to embody the brand values in their interactions with customers and build the kind of customer loyalty that every marketer is ultimately striving for.

WINNING SUPPORT FROM THE TOP

It is impossible to develop an effective long-term employer brand strategy without a clear mandate and proactive support from the leadership team. Without this senior support an employer brand approach is unlikely to carry the authority or attract the resource required to give the proposition real substance. The arguments and the evidence cited above should help in the construction of a business case, but we would also like to share a number of further tips that may help in delivering this case to the CEO and management board:

1. Frame the employer brand strategy in terms that the senior team will recognise. For example, if they are likely to have a relatively narrow view of 'branding', use simpler and more direct expressions such as 'reputation' and 'employee motivation'.
2. Lobby in advance to identify who you can count on for support, and the most likely objections and counter-arguments.
3. Identify the challenges that the strategy will help you to address (e.g. poor external image, difficulty in attracting talent, low employee morale, poor retention).
4. Demonstrate how the strategy links into the overall business plan, and will help to deliver against key goals and targets.
5. Explain how it will complement (and help to coordinate) the other HR, marketing and communications initiatives that are already in progress.

6. Provide benchmark evidence identifying how this approach has benefited other companies (particularly your competitors).
7. Make a realistic assessment of what you hope to achieve in terms of cost savings or added value, and identify the metrics you will use to measure success.
8. Clarify the investment in time and money required to deliver the strategy and your expected return on investment.
9. Dramatise the benefits of success (even the most hard-nosed investment decision involves an element of 'gut feel' and emotional engagement).
10. Demonstrate the role that an employer brand programme can play in reinforcing the leadership credentials of the top team (particularly as 'pathfinders' within an extended group of companies).

Ultimately, there is an element of faith in making the business case for the employer brand. One HR director, formerly a marketing director, pointed out the parallel with advertising:

> I remember attending an advertising conference where one of the speakers said: 'The only thing that is ever certain about advertising is how much it is going to cost you.' It's the same thing here, but nobody would seriously suggest that as a reason for not advertising.

Throughout our research, there appeared to be a general belief that to invest in activities designed to promote greater employee engagement, senior management teams required a far more stringent level of proof than they required for other business activities. There was also a sense of frustration that the default position for many CEOs is to pay more attention to the short-term cost benefits of reducing head count than to the long-term value of building employer brand equity. Conversely, most charismatic leaders, such as Richard Branson, or Charles Dunstone of The Carphone Warehouse, were praised for espousing the power of their people to make a difference, whether they have hard evidence or not. It is our belief that the most successful companies have been those who invest in building high levels of employee engagement, while their competitors are still waiting for the evidence to emerge. If they are not careful, the evidence for those that wait too long may be their own demise.

SUMMARY

1. Strong employer brands increase an organisation's ability to attract, retain and engage people. They also support the organisation's ability to deliver a consistent customer brand experience.
2. There is significant research evidence to suggest that strong employer brands help to reduce the costs associated with recruitment, staff turnover and sickness-absence.
3. Improving employee engagement and commitment to your employer brand is strongly associated with higher levels of customer satisfaction.
4. Organisations with higher levels of employee engagement are also strongly linked with higher revenues, profit margins and overall returns on investment.
5. Effective employer brand management offers a range of different benefits to organisations at every stage of their life cycle.
6. The Human Resources, Marketing and Communications functions can all benefit from a more coordinated approach to developing and managing the employer brand.

Employer Brand Insights 8

The world's most powerful brands are built on great insights into the human condition, but as anyone in marketing soon recognises, there is far more to developing and managing a successful brand than understanding customers' needs and aspirations. When I started my career as a market researcher I recall a well-worn marketing director advising me: 'If all you did was respond to what customers asked of you, you'd soon go out of business.' As my experience extended into marketing consultancy I eventually realised that this sentiment was not driven by hubris, but humility in the face of the complex, multilayered varieties of insight required to successfully manage a brand. To get it right, the brand owner must not only listen carefully to what customers say they need, but must also find a way of understanding their latent and implicit needs (that is to say, the needs they have difficulty expressing or are simply unaware of). In addition to understanding the customer the brand owner must also understand the overall shape, size and dynamics of the market; the underlying organisational or technical capabilities supporting the brand's competitive edge; the investment required to launch and sustain the brand; and how this fits within the overall investment portfolio and business goals of the organisation.

Within the employer brand context we believe that there is significant value in taking a similarly multifaceted approach. Understanding the explicit needs and aspirations of your employees is a good starting point but it is not enough to ensure an effective internal brand strategy. As with customers you also need to develop an understanding of employees' implicit needs, and the organisational, cultural and labour market context within which the employer brand will operate.

Before developing an employer brand strategy we suggest that you need to address the following key questions:

1. How will a stronger employer brand support the business strategy? (Refer to 'The Business Case', Chapter 7.)

2. What kind of employer brand strategy will support the leadership agenda? (Refer to 'The role of leadership', Chapter 5.)

3. What are the main factors currently driving employee engagement and commitment?

4. What kind of organisational culture do you have? How consistent is it across geographical and divisional boundaries?

5. What do employees currently regard as particularly characteristic of and distinctive about the organisation? Is there a consistent core of opinion that is shared by all employees?

6. Do people have a strong sense of the organisation's purpose and values (both implicit and explicit)? How much of a gap is there between the stated ideology of the company and what people actually experience?

7. What behaviours are felt to be most characteristic of the organisation? What are the 'moments of truth' when your organisation is at its best (and worse)?

8. What is the most useful way of segmenting the employee population in terms of their cultural characteristics or distinctive needs?

9. What are the most effective channels of employee communication, both top-down and bottom-up?

10. What kind of employees does your organisation most value and need, now and for the future?

11. What are the main requirements of these target groups in the context of the external labour market?

12. What are the most consistently attractive and compelling organisational attributes for both current employees and potential recruits?

The remainder of the chapter seeks to provide the most effective way of answering these questions, by providing a range of appropriate research techniques.

EMPLOYEE INSIGHTS

As Simon pointed out in Chapter 4, a rough estimation of UK investment in employee research compared with market research suggests that approximately 10 times more is spent on understanding consumers than employees. The total membership of the UK's Market Research Society is 8000. The Employment Research Group that provides a forum for MRS members interested in employee research contains no more than 150. Why is this? It's probably not that most companies value their customers more than their employees, though, as Tesco found in the late 1990s, that is often how employees feel. Experience suggests that it is because management teams believe they already understand their employees, at least enough to manage them effectively. A leading research provider once suggested to me that the objective of most employee research is not to understand employees but to measure them. This may be too extreme a distinction since sophisticated analyses of quantitative data can certainly deliver important insight; however, there is probably an element of truth in this. There is a tendency for managers to use survey data like the proverbial drunk uses the lamp-post, more for support than illumination. Most surveys continue to focus on relatively generic factors like the quality of management, teamwork, training and development, communication, etc. The emphasis is generally placed on identifying and fixing areas of below-average performance. Far more is spent on measuring *what* people think than understanding *why*. In medical parlance, this is more akin to keeping an eye on the vital signs (heartbeat, blood pressure) than developing a fully rounded understanding of what it will take to deliver peak performance.

From the perspective of the marketing insight specialist, the standard employee research toolkit appears very limited. Most organisations continue to conduct an employee survey no more than once a year. Focus groups tend to be used to throw additional light on particularly thorny issues. This ad hoc research is sometimes combined with other sources of continuous data, like sickness-absence, staff turnover and exit interviews. This compares with sophisticated marketing research users such as Unilever, who identify over 25 different sources of insight in their standard market research toolkit, not counting the additional tools they have designed specifically to combine and distil different sources of insight into a coherent platform for action.

We are not suggesting that the employee research budget should match the customer research budget, or that the approaches used to understand employees are exactly equivalent to those used to understand customers and consumers. However, to establish the kind of insights required to develop an effective employer brand, we believe it is worth considering the use of a broader palette of research tools than the conventional employee survey.

Employee Engagement and Commitment

For a long period of time most employee research surveys focused on employee satisfaction. The problem with satisfaction is that it is rather a vague term. Claiming you are satisfied could cover a very broad spectrum from complacency ('I'm satisfied because my job is comfortable and undemanding') to commitment ('I'm satisfied because I've found an organisation I really believe in'). Clearly, most organisations would rather have satisfaction at the commitment end of this spectrum, so most employee surveys have now shifted their focus to defining and measuring more performance-oriented terms such as employee 'commitment' or employee 'engagement'. The issue in shifting the emphasis to these new terms is that they are more difficult to measure directly. While most employees are likely to have no difficulty in stating whether they are satisfied or not with the company they are working for, they are less likely to be able to respond as directly to questions about their level of engagement or commitment. For this reason, these measures tend to be composite terms deriving from a series of other more specific questions. While there is a large amount of published research covering the differences between engagement and commitment, there is still a lack of common agreement over exactly what they mean. Of the five major benchmark studies into this area that we consulted before writing this book, three focused on the term 'engagement' (ISR, Towers Perrin, IES) and two on the term 'commitment' (TNS, Watson Wyatt), but the definition of these terms covered very similar ground.[1-5] Most are composite definitions, drawn from the following:

- Support for the goals and values of the organisation (ISR, TP)
- Belief in the organisation's products/services (IES)
- Sense of pride and belonging (ISR, IES, WW)
- Satisfaction with the immediate job or career prospects (TP, WW, TNS)

- Willingness to go the extra mile (ISR, TP, IES)
- Advocating the employer to others (ISR, TP, WW)
- Intention to stay (ISR, TNS).

Within the HR community, 'engagement' currently appears to be the more favoured of these two terms. From an employer brand perspective, both terms are equally acceptable for summarising an employee's relationship with their employer, as long as the scope of the term (in terms of the contributory factors, featured above) is clearly defined and communicated. However, it may still be worth differentiating the two terms when conducting further analysis. Engagement is generally regarded as a more immediate state (more like the weather than the climate), whereas commitment suggests a more enduring belief in the company. It is possible for an engaged employee to lack longer term commitment, and for a committed employee to feel temporarily disengaged. My benchmark reference point for this is the BBC, where it appears typical for many employees to express a long-term vocational commitment to the BBC as an institution, while feeling continual disenchantment with the way the BBC works as an organisation.

Benchmarking

Once you have defined and measured employee engagement within your organisation, the first question that the senior management team will generally ask is: 'How good or bad is that compared with other organisations?' Many of the large, well-established employee research agencies, such as ISR, have developed an impressive databank of normative benchmarks, and can tell you how your scores compare with your industry peer group, and the more general, but also more testing, index for high-performing companies.

While there may be some issues in comparing like with like, there are also some published benchmarks for engagement according to region and business sectors, which can provide you with a general guide. The first of these (Figure 8.1) is taken from a global study by TNS (2002) involving 20 000 workers across 33 countries.[4]

The sample set of national benchmarks in Figure 8.2 is taken from a global study conducted by ISR (2004) involving 160 000 employees from 10 of the world's largest economies.[1]

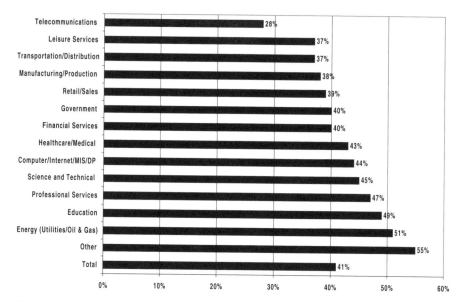

Figure 8.1 How commitment compares across business sectors. *Source:* TNS (2002)

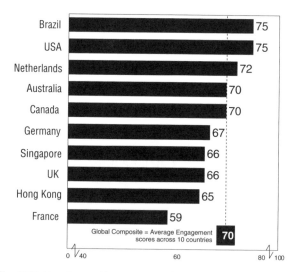

Figure 8.2 The ISR Employee Engagement Index, variations by country: *Source:* ISR (2005)

Another approach to benchmarking is to take part in one of the many 'Best Employers' surveys that have been established over recent years. The two most popular are: *The Sunday Times: 100 Best Companies to Work For*, and the *Financial Times: Best Workplaces* (in the UK and EU). These surveys provide the opportunity for your organisation to enter a league table of employers, all of whom are rated according to a short employee questionnaire, and a separate management submission, usually completed by the HR team. Whether you make it onto the league table or not, every organisation that takes part receives a customised benchmark report showing how you compare in relation to the others.

This can be an easy and cost-effective way of establishing your engagement and employment performance ratings, particularly for small to medium-sized organisations that may lack the financial resources to employ one of the major employee research agencies.

Correlation Analysis

One of my favourite research quotes is: '*I don't drink Guinness because of the advertising; I drink it because it's good for me.*' (The advertising tagline for many years was '*Guinness is good for you*'.) While this quote may be apocryphal, it illustrates one of the central truths of good research, that people are often unaware of (or unprepared to admit) what drives their behaviour. Another classic example is the political polling question: '*Would you vote for the party that raises taxes to support greater investment in health and education?*' The answer to this question is invariably 'yes', however, the results from party elections would strongly suggest that people's behaviour when it comes to casting their votes is somewhat different. The point is that to understand the factors that attract people to an organisation, motivate them to perform at their best, and explain why they leave, you often need more than direct answers to direct questions.

Correlation analysis seeks to identify the factors driving 'key performance indicators' such as employee engagement, commitment and loyalty, by establishing their statistical correlation with other questions (confidence in leadership, good internal communication, etc.). In simple terms, if 90% of the employees expressing strong commitment to the organisation also claim a high degree of confidence in the leadership team, and similarly, most people expressing low commitment claim low confidence in the leadership, then it is fair to assume that leadership is an important factor in driving employee commitment.

We will cover some of the results from recent benchmark studies in the next chapter on the employer brand proposition, but some of the most pioneering work in this field has been conducted by the employee research consultancy ISR. In a global study involving 360 000 employees from 41 companies (2001), ISR identified the four major factors driving organisational commitment as being: (i) quality of leadership, (ii) opportunities for development, (iii) empowerment and (iv) the people management skills of employee's immediate managers.[6]

Continuous Research

Since it is now commonplace for employees to be described in terms of human capital or assets, it is surprising how many organisations conduct an employee survey only once a year, bi-annually or even less frequently. It would be regarded as foolhardy to check your organisation's financial status no more than once a year, so why is a more continuous approach to employee research so uncommon? We suspect this is because employee research is seldom regarded as business as usual. It is regarded as an additional effort, no doubt necessary, but nevertheless a potential interruption to everyday business, involving a large input of data that needs to be collected, analysed, digested and responded to. It feels more like an initiative than a regular feature of the way the organisation is managed. This is not how most businesses research their customers and consumers. The great benefit of adopting a more continuous approach is that you can develop a far better understanding of how employees are responding to events over time. Change is a constant feature of most organisations, and taking an annual snapshot of employee opinion can be rather a hit-and-miss affair. The context within which an ad hoc survey is conducted will seldom match the conditions of the previous survey. An organisation can never be sure of the degree to which it is recording employees' responses to changes since the last survey or the more immediate context within which the survey is taking place.

As our client John Lewis discovered when we helped them establish a continuous survey process in 2003, seeking people's views on a more continuous basis also enables the senior team to identify and respond to issues much more quickly. When levels of employee engagement begin to fall the effect on performance is sometimes delayed. By the time the problem shows up in the financial numbers, the issues driving the downturn have often taken root, and are far more difficult to rectify. Rather than disrupting the business, this approach makes employee research a regular feature of business as usual, enabling the management team to pick up and address issues as they arise and avoid the indigestible backlog of issues often associated with less frequent surveys.

The other more specific benefit of continuous research is that it makes it easier to match employee data with customer satisfaction and sales data. Many organisations have found that establishing the link between employee engagement, customer satisfaction and sales/profitability can be an extremely valuable exercise in that it helps to quantify the return on the organisation's investment in people management. As we mentioned in the previous chapter, this linkage has become a regular feature in many retail businesses, and is now being picked up across a wide range of other industry sectors.

Culture Mapping

Employee surveys tend to be used to measure the people management performance of the organisation and, in conjunction with correlation analysis, can provide a good indication of the factors most likely to be driving employee engagement. However, conventional surveys tend to be less effective at identifying the longer term cultural characteristics of the organisation. You may find from a conventional survey that your score for teamwork is generally low. What it is less likely to be able to tell you is whether this is the result of a specific management intervention (like performance management), a training issue (poor team management skills), or a more deeply rooted cultural characteristic ('this company has always favoured individualism').

If you are setting out to strengthen the employer brand it is important to understand not only the immediate 'climate' of employee opinion, but also the longer term culture of the organisation. Culture, like personality, is often a difficult concept to define precisely, because it describes general patterns and tendencies rather than a reliable objective reality. Nevertheless, like brand personality, the notion of organisational culture can be very useful in getting a handle on how people generally perceive the organisation works. What do people regard as normal within the context of the organisation? What kind of behaviour tends to be rewarded or frowned upon? What kind of people tend to do well within the organisation, or struggle to fit in? These are particularly useful questions to ask if you are trying to define and develop the employer brand, because the culture of the organisation is a good way of describing the current brand reality, as opposed to its value statements, which tend to be more closely related to the brand vision. More simply put, culture is descriptive (the way things are); values are aspirational (the way things should be).

One of the commonest ways of researching organisational culture is to present people with a series of bipolar scales describing the general preferences of the organisation. Each employee is asked to provide an opinion on how the collective people within the organisation tend to think and act, rather than how he or she, personally, tends to think and act. (Asking for both perspectives can be valuable in providing additional insight into the level of fit between employees and the organisational culture.)

There are a number of standardised cultural frameworks that can be used for this purpose. Two of the most widely used are Geert Hofstede's 5-D model[7] and Fons Trompenaars' seven-dimensional model.[8] The main focus of both these models is cross-cultural diversity within multinational organisations; nevertheless they can still provide a useful starting point for mapping any organisation. The following summarises some of the most common dimensions used in models of this kind:

Inner directed/organisational focus	vs	Outer directed/customer focus
Past/stability	vs	Future/change
Risk averse/incremental	vs	Risk taking/creative innovation
Short term/operational reality	vs	Long-term/strategic vision
People/relationships	vs	Performance/transactions
Individualism/stars	vs	Collectivism/team
Rules/process	vs	Flexibility/results
Hierarchy/title	vs	Meritocracy/task
Control/top-down	vs	Empowerment/involvement
Rational/analytical	vs	Intuitive/'gut feel'
Formal/reserved	vs	Informal/emotive

The purpose of this mapping exercise is to provide the organisation with a more explicit framework for measuring the cultural tendencies of the organisation. This can help to identify the potential gap between where you are (brand reality) and where you need to be (brand vision) to achieve your organisational goals. It provides a valuable context for reviewing current values or developing new values by identifying the degree of resonance or dissonance with the current culture. It also helps to determine the degree of cultural consistency across geographies, divisions and operating units. Does the organisation have widespread commonalities? Where are the dividing lines? This exercise is particularly useful in the context of a merger or acquisition where two potentially different corporate cultures are being brought together.

Brand Roots

Mapping the broad cultural characteristics of the organisation will only take you so far. This exercise may help you to determine the 'type' of organisation you have, but not what makes it unique. If you think of it in terms of understanding each employee, the knowledge that some are extrovert, intuitive, thinkers and judgers (following the Myers–Briggs dimensions) could be very helpful in working out how best to manage them, but it won't be enough to define any one as a unique individual.[9] If you were describing a colleague to a friend, you'd be a lot more specific. You're more likely to say something like: 'She's a real northerner, down to earth, calls a spade a spade, spends a lot of time up mountains, and despite her slim build, she never stops eating.' In other words, you would focus much more on what makes her different. Where she's from. How she tends to express herself. The kinds of thing she likes doing. From an employer brand perspective it's useful to understand both the type of culture you have (for the purpose of general positioning), and the specific elements of history and 'personality' that differentiate your organisation from every other.

So where do you look to find what makes your organisation unique? To begin with we suggest you conduct a bit of desk research. Brand managers tend to start their stewardship with an induction into the history of the brand. This helps them to understand the brand's roots, the story of its origin, and the key milestones in its history. I recently picked up a leaflet celebrating the 75th anniversary of the tea brand PG Tips, and learned that the 'Tips' referred to the top two leaves and bud of the tea plant from which the product was originally derived. I also found out that blue and green have been the brand colours since it was very first introduced in 1930 and that the chimps' advertisement, first screened in 1956, was the longest-running TV campaign in the UK. This kind of information puts the brand into context. It helps to identify what is deep-rooted and authentic, and provides important insights into the character and personality of the brand. This kind of exercise is equally valuable for employer brands. What's the organisation's story? Where and how did it start? What significant events have shaped the organisation over the course of its history? For some longstanding organisations there are published histories. Weighing up the differences between the official, authorised versions and unauthorised 'inside story' accounts can be particularly revealing. For most others you will have to do some digging. If there is no official archive, the best place to start is talking to the 'elders' within the organisation, long-serving employees 'who remember the early days'. It's surprising how often you can find an unofficial archivist, if you can't locate an official store of historical memorabilia. While we would not suggest you need to write a full history of the organisation, establishing some of the key dates, personalities and 'moments of truth' for the organisation can provide valuable depth to your understanding of the current employer brand, and some useful material for your induction process.

Projective and Enabling Techniques

The second route we suggest in identifying the unique characteristics of an organisation is to conduct workshop-style employee focus groups. The focus in this case is *not* their views on more immediate issues such as the latest business strategy, the quality of their local management or their personal needs, but *more general* observations about the organisation as a whole. It is often useful to divide these sessions between recent joiners and longer serving employees. Recent joiners can offer a relatively fresh perspective on the way the organisation seems to work, as well as insight into the gaps between their early experience of the organisation and their external expectations as candidates. Longer serving employees bring a wider range of experience, and are generally more able to differentiate between the official line ('this is what we're meant to say') and the inside story ('but this is the way it really works').

In consumer research it is common to use what are called projective and enabling techniques (such as personification and role playing) to explore thoughts and feelings that people often find difficult to express in response to direct questioning. We have found these to be extremely useful in the context of employer brand research, as people often find it difficult to provide a full and rich response to direct questions about the personality or culture of their current organisation. One of the reasons for this is that culture tends to be assumed and implicit, and it is often difficult for someone within a culture to describe it objectively. For long-serving employees especially, the way in which things work appears self-evidently normal, and it is difficult for them to describe what is different or unique about it. The other great benefit of using these techniques is that people find them a lot more energising and stimulating than your average focus group.

The following represents a selection of the exercises that we have found useful in providing both great insights into how people perceive the employer brand, and a rich and stimulating source of outputs for illustrating the key findings of the research.

Sunny Side Up

- *Best of*: What would you put in the advert to present the very best of what the organisation can offer?
- *Heroes:* Who would appear in the organisation's hall of fame and why?
- *Legend:* How would Disney tell the organisation's story if they made it into a film?
- *Greatest hits:* What records would you choose for a celebratory party album?
- *Perfect day:* Describe a perfect working day.

The Shadow Side

- *Rough guide:* What don't they tell you at induction that you need to know to survive and prosper?
- *Villains:* Who are the black sheep of the organisation, and why?
- *Obituary:* What would be written on the organisation's tombstone if it went out of business in the next few years?
- *Hell:* What would be the key characteristics of a typically hellish day?

Personification

- *Personality* – If the organisation were represented by a single person, what type of person would that be? (It often helps to start with a few iconic examples, like Marks & Spencer, Nike or McDonalds to warm people up.) Once people have entered the spirit of this exercise you can also ask a series of more specific questions like: What kind of car would they drive? What kind of paper would they read? What kind of pets would they keep? etc.
- *Employer vs customer brand* – If the employer brand name is the same as the product/service brand, divide the group in two, and ask one subgroup to focus on the employer brand, and the other the customer brand (as they would expect customers to see it).
- *Brand party* – Repeat the above exercise for a number of your main rivals, and then describe what would happen if they all met at a party. Describe how they would behave. Who would get on with whom? Who would dance all night? Who would spend the whole night talking in the kitchen? etc.
- *Celebrity* – Who would be the most appropriate celebrity to represent the organisation as it would like to see itself? And as it actually is?
- *Organisational stereotypes* – How would you describe a typical cast of employees from the organisation?

Summary

We suggest that these techniques are used to elicit people's open and spontaneous perceptions of the organisation before any pre-prepared stimuli are introduced, such as recruitment materials, proposition statements, or values. The reason for this is to clearly differentiate between the employer brand reality as it currently exists in people's heads, and the more formalised statements represented by the current or potential employer brand vision. When you prompt people on the values of the organisation, a useful technique is to ask them to consider 'moments of truth' for each value. To take an external example, a typical moment of truth for a service brand is when something goes wrong. Your baggage doesn't turn up at the airport you're flying to. The air conditioning isn't working in the hotel you've booked into on a stiflingly hot day. How does the company offering the service respond? That is the moment of truth.

For an organisation that states 'transparency' as a value, the moment of truth comes when something has gone wrong and you want to find out what's going on. For an organisation that claims 'respect' as a value, it is how the organisation deals with an operationally successful manager who is consistently disrespectful to employees.

One further line of enquiry that can be very useful in diagnosing the underlying dynamics of the employer brand is to ask how people perceive the organisation to be changing over time, through such questions as:

• What symbolises the past? What seems to be on the way out?
• What most represents the 'here and now', or 'the flavour of the moment'?
• What are the emerging signs of the future? What seems to be on the way in?

Through these exercises you are searching for the significant stories that people tell about the organisation: the language and metaphors they use, and aspects of the corporate body language they believe to be symbolic of the way things work. You're looking for the characteristics of the organisation that energise the employees and give them pride – that is, the 'passion points' that strike an emotional chord with people. You're also looking for the tensions between corporate rhetoric (the way things are supposed to be) and the everyday reality (the way things really are), particularly at those moments of truth when a key value or corporate belief is put the test.

Observation

One of the simplest forms of organisational research is to take an outsider's perspective and simply observe the way in which the organisation operates. This will generally require a trained, external observer; however, there are a number of simple techniques that you could try for yourselves. The first of these is to try to describe what you see as if you were an anthropologist recording the habits and rituals of a strange tribal culture. Before you start, try this exercise. Take off your watch and put it in your pocket. Then draw the face of your watch in as much detail as you can. Despite the fact you have probably looked at your watch hundreds of times, most people find this task quite difficult. That is the difference between *looking* and actively *seeing*. With this in mind, here is a short checklist for taking a fresh look at the organisation around you. In each case describe what you see, then try and draw some conclusions about what you think it signifies about the organisation.

- *Public spaces* – External architecture. Reception areas.
- *Working environment* – Arrangement of space. Expressions of hierarchy. Shared vs private. Open vs closed. Neat vs cluttered. Use of wall space.
- *Comfort zones* – Coffee facilities. Canteens. Toilets.
- *Dress codes* – Formal vs informal. Degree of conformity. Expression of hierarchy.
- *Meetings* (both large and small) – Time keeping. Allocation of time to telling, listening, discussing, generating ideas, making decisions.
- *Social events* – Seasonal celebrations. Ad hoc celebrations. Leaving parties.

Segmentation

Most of the approaches we have described above set out to discover what is common among employees, their shared needs, motivations, perceptions and values. However, most organisations are diverse, and are generally seeking to become more diverse. In addition to finding the common ground, it is therefore necessary to determine an effective way of responding to this diversity. Segmentation is a tool used to identify the most significant and meaningful way of dividing people into groups who can be catered for differently according to their specific needs. There is a practical limit to segmentation, since the benefit of addressing individual groups is soon outweighed by the cost if the target group is too small, or the total number of target groups too great. This is an important factor to consider in the context of employees, where the potential criteria for segmentation (age, sex, level, function, region, psychographic profile, etc.) can often appear as numerous as the employees themselves. In some obvious respects, some form of segmentation is already inherent in such common features of employment as pay scales and job grades. However, a number of companies have begun to push the concept of segmentation further (see the Tesco case study – Appendix 2), and we believe the application of this technique is likely to grow in both frequency and sophistication over the coming years.

One of the most useful forms of segmentation is to cluster people according to the level and primary focus of their engagement. For example, the TNS commitment survey conducted in 2002 and 2004 measured commitment on two axes: commitment to the organisation, and commitment to people's career, or type of work.[4] The four main segments this analysis produced were as follows:

- **Ambassadors** (41%), defined as those fully committed to their company and to their work/career. (Tend to be mid to upper managers and high performers.)

  Primary commitment drivers:
  Performance management/achievement
  - Company has an effective system for evaluating performance.
  - My ability to achieve and to move the company forward is a key reason why I work here.
  Leadership
  - I have strong confidence in the leadership of this company.
  - I have strong confidence in my department leadership

- **Career Oriented** (20%), defined as those more dedicated to their career than to their company. (Also tend to be top performers, but looking for training and development to improve their skills.)

  Primary commitment drivers:
  Work culture/empowerment
  - I have the opportunity to do what I do best every day.
  - I have control over the way I work.
  - I have sufficient authority to carry out my job effectively.
  Performance management
  - I know what I need to be successful at my job.
  - I have a clear understanding of how my job performance is judged.

- **Company Oriented** (8%), defined as those whose commitment to the company surpasses their commitment to their work and career. (Solid corporate citizens, with solid skill set but limited talent.)

  Primary commitment drivers:
  The company overall
  - People at work have a real interest in my well-being.
  - My company's a fun place to work.

- I feel valued as an employee.
- My company has good physical working conditions.
Fairness
- Procedure for considering employees for job openings is fair.
- All employees are given equal opportunity.

- **Ambivalent** (31%), defined as those who are committed to neither their company nor their career. (Tend to be low talent/low skill.)

Communication Audits

It is essential for any brand manager to develop a sophisticated understanding of the range of channels that are available, and which are the most effective for different target audiences or different types of message. In this external context, in addition to delivering a specific message or packet of information, every piece of communication the customer receives is also designed to reinforce the overall brand proposition. We believe that an equally sophisticated understanding is required for internal channels if the employer brand is going to perform a similar role for internal communication. (This is a subject we will explore further in a later chapter.) In auditing the current communication framework we believe that the employer brand manager needs answers to the following series of questions.

- *Sources* – How, when and from whom is the content for internal corporate communication currently sourced? Is the current range of sources providing the information required? Do you have the right mix of sources? Too many sources? Too few? Are they being provided with clear information about their responsibilities?
- *Content* – How do you currently segment the information you communicate in terms of type (strategy, news, social, etc.), relevance (corporate, divisional, unit specific, etc.), importance (priority, for reference, etc.) or response required (action this day!, provide feedback, cascade, etc.)? Do you have the right balance of content? To what extent is the content currently aligned?
- *Editorial control* – Who has responsibility for editorial control or message management and for what types of information? How effective is editorial control in aligning communication with a

common agenda? How effective is it in filtering communication for relevance? Is there sufficient air-traffic control to avoid information overload?

- *Audiences* – How do you currently segment your audiences? How could you segment your audiences to improve the relevance and effectiveness of your communication? What are the primary needs of each audience? Are the key audiences getting what they need and want?
- *Transmission channels* – What channels are currently available (including face to face)? How and when are they used both in terms of sending and receiving communication? Are key audiences getting the information they need through the channels they prefer? Is the right mix of channels being deployed to get the information through?
- *Feedback channels* – What channels are currently available? How and when are they used? Are the current feedback channels accessible, regular enough and effective enough to provide good quality response and input to decision makers?
- *Response/action* – Who has responsibility for filtering and responding to feedback? Is feedback receiving sufficient recognition and responsive action?

Additional Sources

In addition to these research-specific channels, there are a number of further potential sources of insight that can prove valuable to explore.

Leavers' Interviews

Well conducted and consistently reported leavers' interviews can shed valuable light on engagement and retention issues.

Performance and Development Reviews

These can be particularly useful in tracking the uptake of value-related behaviours. Managers should also be encouraged to report on regular patterns of response that may suggest new and emerging issues.

Sickness-Absence and Health Screening

Indications of stress within the company can provide a useful counter-indicator to positive engagement. In some cases, this kind of unhealthy stress can also exist at the opposite end of the engagement spectrum. In a high-commitment, high-performance culture, widespread stress symptoms and growing levels of sickness-absence can indicate the need to reign in the number of hours people devote to the organisation to ensure that performance remains sustainable. This was such a common issue in Japan that some years ago the government introduced a major campaign to ensure that people took their holidays.

LABOUR MARKET INSIGHTS

The main factors driving retention and motivation are not necessarily going to be the same factors that drive the desirability of the company to potential employees. For this reason, it is also important to conduct research into the labour market from which the company will be seeking to recruit. The phrase 'war for talent' has been used to dramatise the increasing difficulty many employers have experienced over recent years in attracting people of the right quality to meet the needs of their business. This is not just a question of attracting 'top talent' for management positions, but finding people with the right mix of qualities to successfully perform a wide variety of roles throughout the organisation.

Ensuring the 'right fit' is also as important as attracting high quality. Getting the employer brand proposition right is just as much an exercise in targeting the right kind of candidates for employment as ensuring that you have a large number to choose from. During an economic downturn, when more people are competing for employment, it could be argued that employer brand becomes less important. However, in ensuring that the company stays focused in targeting and attracting the right kind of candidates, the discipline that an employer brand approach brings to the recruitment process can be more essential than ever.

From an employer brand research perspective we suggest the following steps.

Clarifying the Target Market

Defining and segmenting the target market is often the first essential step in effective brand development and management. In the employer brand context, the overall target profile often starts with a definition of the values and attitudes that the organisation is looking for in all of its employees. If you are truly seeking to 'live the brand' it helps if your employees already share the core values of the organisation. A secondary consideration, which is now becoming more common, is recruiting for diversity. This may sound as if it conflicts with the agenda for shared values, but the kind of values and attitudes that most organisations are looking for tend to be well distributed across the range of different groups generally considered under the heading of diversity. This need not mean positive discrimination according to gender, ethnic background, sexual orientation or disability, but it may determine where and how you seek to advertise for candidates.

The second stage is then to segment the market according to levels of experience and the types of skills and competencies you are looking for. This need not be exhaustive, but it helps to map out the sources of talent from which you are most often seeking recruits – for example, graduates, front-line service personnel, professional managers, functional specialists (e.g. Marketing, IT, Engineering). If you are clear about the main target groups, it becomes a lot easier to conduct further research into the distinctive needs and aspirations of each group, and their awareness and perceptions of your organisation. It also becomes easier to monitor your success in attracting the right kind of recruits. What proportion of candidates match your ideal profile? What are the relative application and acceptance rates among each group?

Needs and Aspirations

Once you have defined and segmented your target market the next step is to identify the most important factors in determining your target groups' choice of employer. In external marketing research you generally start with the basic 'tablestakes' required to attract people, then progress to a more specific analysis of individual subgroups. Some of the most obvious tablestakes in employment include a basic demonstration of trust and respect, but there may be a number of growing tendences that will cause you to judge more carefully. For example, does the growing interest in work–life balance mean that some form of flexible working should now be offered to all employees? How should you respond to growing expectation that even the humblest of employees should be able to participate in some form of self-development? There are a great many studies to choose from in making this general assessment. McKinsey's seminal study 'The War for Talent'[10] still holds many relevant insights into attracting talented people into every level of the organisation, and if you are looking for a more down-to-earth and acerbic commentary on the subject you should try Mike Johnson's *Talent Magnet*.[11]

Having established the baseline, the next step is to consider the more specific needs and aspirations of individual target groups. There are some published studies that have looked at specific groups, such as graduates, and could provide you with a starting point, but in most cases you're going to have to conduct your own research. The most cost-effective place to start is with your own employees. A number of organisations have begun to conduct Joiner's Surveys or focus groups, which can provide some very useful insights into the criteria used by different types of employee to make their choice. Some companies, such as Warner, have taken this a step further by setting up regular under-30s staff forums to explore what modern job-seekers are looking for from organisations.

Conducting research among current employees will clearly provide only a partial view of a target group's needs and aspirations, as it will be biased towards those who were positively disposed towards the organisation. It is useful, therefore, to incorporate a number of these key questions into the recruitment process itself to identify unmet needs that may be leading to rejection. Recent research from the recruitment firm Reed claimed that two-thirds of people have turned down new job offers, and with growing levels of employee confidence, evaluating rejection is becoming an increasingly critical component in understanding the competitive dynamics of the marketplace.

For particularly important, or difficult to recruit, target groups, such as engineers, it may also be worth while conducting more targeted surveys, focus groups and individual interviews in the marketplace. While this can be both difficult and expensive to organise, the benefit in terms of getting the proposition right for these groups can be significant.

Employer Brand Image

It is common for product or service brand marketers to use some form of brand relationship ladder that starts with basic awareness, and progresses through trial, and repeat purchase to brand loyalty and active brand advocacy. This is an interesting concept to apply to the employer brand, although it involves a number of additional dimensions. In the context of employment we suggest that it would be useful to have a viewpoint on the answers to the following questions in relation to each target group:

- *Name Recognition* – How many people are likely to recognise the name of the organisation?
- *Awareness* – Of the people that recognise the name of the organisation, how many are likely to have a reasonably accurate idea of what the organisation does? What is generally known about the organisation's products or services? What is generally known about the size, scope and success of the business? What, if anything, is known about the organisation's employment record and practices?
- *Saliency* – How many people in the target group would consider your organisation if they were seeking a new employer? What are people's general perceptions of you as a potential employer? To what extent is this answer based on general perceptions of the industry sector or organisational type? Which other organisations would people include in their 'wish list' of employment preferences?
- *Trial* – What are the leading reasons for making an application? What impression of your organisation is given by your recruitment materials and activities? Your website? What, if anything, do people hear about your organisation when they ask around?
- *Brand experience* – What are people's first impressions on joining the organisation? To what extent does it meet with their expectations? What are the most significant gaps between their image of the organisation before joining and their experience?
- *Retention and advocacy* (in addition to the other subjects covered under 'employee insights') – How does people's image of the organisation change as they become more of an insider? What would people tell potential recruits about the organisation?
- *Alumni* – How do people describe the organisation to others once they have left? To what extent do they remain active advocates?

Brand mapping is another common technique that marketers use to understand their relative positioning in the marketplace. It involves presenting people with a variety of brand names on cards or Post-It Notes that they should group according to degrees of similarity. This exercise can usually be performed without much direction, and can be very revealing about how people categorise different types of employer. The exercise can also be conducted in response to a number of relevant prompts – for example, how would you group these brands according to their CV appeal, or level of care towards employees? Even though people may only have a very superficial understanding of the employment practices of each company, it is surprising how readily they can categorise different organisations into general types.

In addition to researching people's perceptions it is also valuable to conduct an analysis of the competitors who tend to turn up in your target market's salient sets. Most organisations' websites incorporate material aimed at prospective employees, and this information, along with their recruitment advertising, can be used to analyse their underlying proposition. It can also be used to compare more specific details about the kind of benefits employees could expect from different organisations.

SUMMARY

1. Just as the most powerful product and service brands are founded on a multifaceted approach to insight building, it is equally important to adopt a wide range of tools and techniques to acquire the insights necessary to develop and manage an effective employer brand.
2. Understanding the key drivers of engagement and commitment is a critical step in helping to define a powerful employment proposition.
3. The 'culture' and 'personality' of your organisation are often the most challenging to make explicit, the most likely to provide sources of differentiation, and the most dangerous to ignore in defining your core values.
4. The best starting point for labour market research is your own most recent recruits, but you need to be mindful of the limitations of this approach.
5. Researching the external labour market is generally more challenging in logistical terms than employee research, but there are a number of useful tools that can be adopted from customer research.
6. The concept of a brand relationship 'ladder' can be a useful way of integrating your labour market insights with your employee research.

Employer Brand Positioning 9

The previous chapter should have provided you with the insight tools you need to identify how the employer brand is currently perceived and experienced (the brand reality) and the kind of employer brand that would improve your appeal to potential recruits, and lead to higher levels of engagement, retention and brand advocacy (the brand vision). The purpose of this chapter is to bring all of these elements together into a brand positioning model that will provide the principal navigational tool for developing and managing the brand experience.

BRAND IDENTITY

The first place to start is to establish the internal positioning of the employer brand. There are three principal kinds of employer brand relating to different positions within the brand identity hierarchy of an organisation.

Monolithic

This is where the organisation uses the same brand name and visual identity throughout all its operations. The brand name that people buy as customers is the same brand name that people work for as employees. Examples include: Tesco, Reuters, HSBC, Nokia and Vodafone. The monolithic employer brand needs to clarify its relationship with the customer brand, and the other key facets of the corporate brand, including vision, purpose, values and public affairs.

Parent

This comes in two versions. In the first version there are two levels of organisation brand, a corporate parent brand and an operating company brand. Examples include: WPP, RBS, Compass and Kingfisher. In this case, the parent employer brand needs to clarify the parameters within which it expects its subsidiary company employer brands to operate. In the second version, the corporate brand provides an umbrella for a number of different product and services brands. Examples include: Unilever and P&G. This type of employer brand needs to work consistently with the other key facets of the corporate brand including vision, purpose, values, trade relationships and public affairs. Increasingly, as in the Unilever example, it also needs to consider the role of consumer brand endorsement.

Subsidiary

This represents the operating company counterpart to the parent brand. The employer brand is typically the same as the customer brand. Examples include: NatWest, Direct Line and Coutts, all of which belong to the Royal Bank of Scotland Group. The subsidiary employer brand needs to clarify its relationship with both the parent brand and the customer brand.

BRAND INTEGRATION (CUSTOMER AND EMPLOYER BRANDS)

Many brand positioning models within service companies are dominated by the customer perspective despite the fact that employees experience the brand in a different way to the customer, and are motivated by different types of benefit. The model shown in Figure 9.1 presents a more integrated approach. To ensure brand integrity, it recognises that some brand qualities need to shine through every stakeholder's experience of the brand, while others need to be specifically designed to meet the different needs and aspirations of customers and employees.

While the customer brand and employer brand compete in two different markets – one for products and services; the other for talent and commitment – they are closely interrelated. The employer brand, in

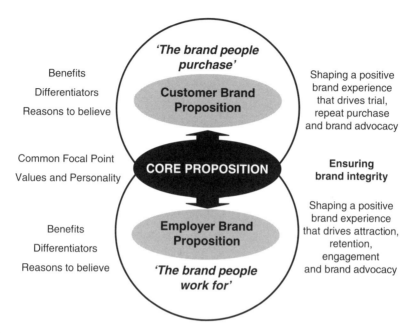

Figure 9.1 An integrated brand model. *Source*: People in Business

attracting the right employees and maintaining their commitment to high performance, plays a critical role in building and supporting the customer brand. Likewise, the strength of the customer brand plays an important role in attracting the right people to come and work for the company. Once employed, the pride they share in the company's external reputation helps in maintaining their loyalty and commitment to delivering on the company's brand promises to its customers. The model helps to clarify these interrelationships and manage them more effectively by providing a more integrated platform for strategic planning and delivery.

CORPORATE BRAND HIERARCHY (PARENT AND SUBSIDIARY)

As any parent will agree, it's difficult to strike the right balance between control and freedom, between encouragement and discipline, between concern and interference. It's no different for the management of a holding company. There are, of course, further issues to consider, such as the benefits of standardisation vs the benefits of local flexibility. While there is a general tendency for corporate parents to seek beneficial synergies, even the most carefully managed global brands, like Coca-Cola, have gone 'glocal' to meet the specific needs of their local markets. Brand consistency provides a powerful advantage in clarifying the brand message, but only up to a point. If brands do not resonate with their local markets, consistency counts for nothing. This is just as true for employer brand management as it is for the customer-facing brand. Where there are two levels of branding, the general rule is to align the employer brand as closely as possible with the customer-facing brand to ensure integrity between the internal and external faces of the brand. Unless, of course, the longer term strategy is to develop a more monolithic brand identity, in which case the employer brand can begin to pave the way from the inside out.

Assuming the longer term corporate strategy is to maintain a two-tier branding structure, we would advise the parent brand to tread relatively lightly in terms of the employer brand values, personality and benefits, and focus on establishing a more generic foundation of shared best practice. There are three main areas in which parental intervention works effectively in this regard. The first is corporate ethics. Very few subsidiary companies would argue against working within a shared framework of sound ethical principles (though our recommendation would be to call them principles and not core values, as this tends to get muddled with local brand values). The second is management training. One of the major benefits of working within a large corporation is the potential headroom it provides for long-term career development, and becoming the management brand is generally a very effective positioning for the corporate employer brand. The third is best practice sharing (not to be confused with standardisation). While management teams constantly defend their own room to manoeuvre, they also tend to be the first to criticise a silo mentality, and providing forums and channels for sharing best practice is probably one of the most popular ways for the parent brand to add value.

The centralisation of HR and the provision of shared services has become an increasingly common approach. It has worked reasonably effectively in monolithic organisations where there is only one employer brand, but we suggest caution in applying it to multiple branded organisations where HR has a key role to play in supporting different local employer brand cultures.

Where parent brands most appear to overstep the mark is in trying to apply corporate values and wholesale programmes of culture change across a wide variety of local operating companies, where the corporate ideology conflicts with the dynamics of the local brand. Even in monolithically branded companies there need to be appropriate degrees of freedom to adapt to the local cultural environment. Ask anyone who works in Europe for a US-based parent company, and they will tell you that this is a constant subject of negotiation. For a parent brand operating in different geographical markets, under different brand names, it is even more of a mistake, or at least a waste of money, because it is very seldom successful.

THE KEY COMPONENTS OF THE POSITIONING MODEL

The following describes one approach to defining your employer brand positioning, but for the sake of internal consistency we would recommend you adapt it to align with the positioning model currently being used for your corporate or customer brand. Since we believe this approach to employer branding can help to fill a gap in most conventional positioning models, we would hope that this process of adaptation works in both directions.

We recommend that you conduct this positioning exercise twice – first for the brand reality and then for the brand vision. Our positioning model (Figure 9.2) is divided in two. The upper section contains the core brand elements (common to all), and the lower section the employee value propositions for more specific target groups.

THE BRAND REALITY MODEL

The purpose of the brand reality model is to summarise how the employer brand is currently perceived and experienced by your key target groups. It is designed to be an aggregate view, describing the organisation as it is commonly viewed, not the organisation at its best or worst. Unless you have a particularly strong external brand image as an employer, we suggest that you confine the reality model to your current employees. If you have a strong external image, we only recommend that you combine internal and external perceptions if they are closely aligned. It

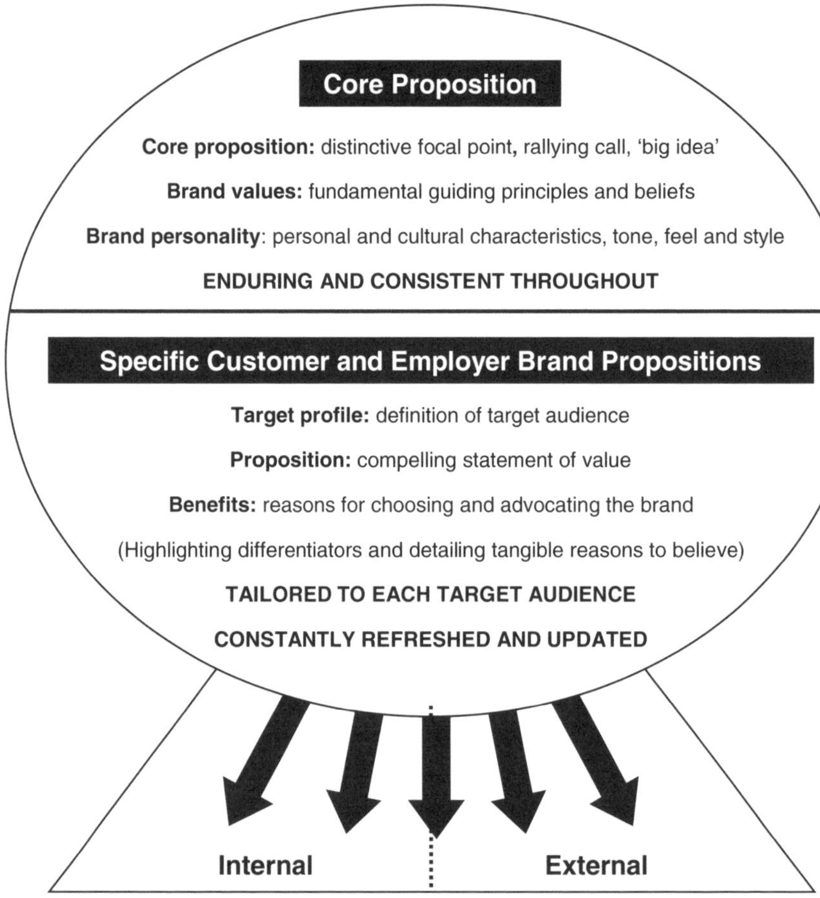

Figure 9.2 The brand platform. *Source*: PiB

is otherwise better to construct two reality models, to help to define any perceptual gaps. This exercise is as much an art as a science, and however much research you have conducted you will still need to make judgements about what is important. Don't try to include every angle. The aim is to distil your description down to the most essential ingredients.

Current Employee Profile

Have you favoured particular types of recruit (particularly at management level)? If so, what is the typical profile of your current employees, and the types of people you are seeking to recruit? This may appear to be a difficult question to answer, but whether the organisation is conscious of it or not, there tends to be a general understanding of the kinds of people who will 'fit in', and it helps to make this explicit when you define your employer brand proposition, and your standpoint on organisational diversity.

Current Employer Brand Proposition

What is the most common reason given for people's commitment and loyalty to the organisation? If a number of common reasons are given, state no more than two or three. If there is very little commonality, state 'Unclear'. If you already have a formally stated employer brand proposition, you should only use it here if it is substantiated by employees.

Current Values and Personality

What are the mostly commonly described characteristics of the organisation? State no more than six to eight in total. Don't worry too much at this stage about discriminating between values and personality traits. They often overlap.

As above, you should only include current formalised value statements if they are spontaneously corroborated by your employees. Be honest. If your employee research suggests any commonly held negative views, include them. To give you an illustration, the HR Director of a City law firm once claimed that the two descriptions most used by employees to describe the organisation's partners were 'arrogance' and 'greed'. In being honest, you may also need to be brave.

Current Benefits

What do employees most commonly describe as the benefits of working for your organisation? This should be a more extensive list than the reasons for commitment defined under the brand proposition. You should also try to differentiate and prioritise the perceived benefits for each of the target groups. We suggest that you focus on the functional benefits ('good pay', 'good career prospects'). While it may be appropriate to include some emotional benefits (such as 'caring') for specific target groups, it is likely that the most common emotional benefits will have already been defined as values or personality traits.

Current Differentiators

Underline the features above which employees most believe differentiate the organisation from others. Does *what* you do provide the most distinctive focus, or *how* you do it?

THE BRAND VISION MODEL

The purpose of the brand vision model is to define the kind of employer brand that the organisation would like to develop to improve your appeal to potential recruits, and lead to higher levels of employee engagement, retention and brand advocacy. It is important to establish your time frame for this model. If you feel that your current offer is a lot stronger than employees perceive it to be, you may set a relatively short time frame, with an emphasis on sharpening your communication of current benefits. If you believe there is a lot more work to be done on the underlying offer, it may be more realistic to set a 3–5 year time frame for realising the employer brand vision. This should also be aligned with the wider context. For an integrated employer/customer brand you will need to consider the time frame within which the customer brand is working. Likewise, the corporate strategy may be working within a given time frame to achieve certain business goals, or to realise a long-term vision.

Target Employee Profiles

It is increasingly common for organisations to define the kind of attitudinal and value profiles that they wish to recruit into the organisation. From a brand perspective, the profile of customer-facing employees is particularly important. Many organisations have stopped trying to force their values onto people with endless pep talks, rigid processes and scripts as this often makes the customer service feel artificial. As Alex Marples of Kaisen commented in relation to his consulting work for Lego: 'Rather than trying to adjust the values to fit the people, our job is to select those who fit the environment . . . you can't force people, it's like chasing water uphill.'[1]

To work effectively this approach needs to be balanced with a healthy dose of diversity, particularly at the management level. In many organisations the problem is not that people don't fit, but that they fit too comfortably with the prevailing organisational view of the world. This can be as equally damaging as attitudinal dissonance with the prevailing values, since creativity and innovation, the lifeblood of long-term business success, are highly dependent on creating an environment in which people feel able to challenge existing norms. There is no easy answer to this paradox. Every organisation needs to make its own judgement on the most effective balance between conformity and diversity, but at the very least it should have the debate, and make its conclusions explicit when it comes to defining the employer brand positioning.

The Employer Brand Proposition

What is the most compelling reason why people should describe your organisation as a great place to work? One of the key benefits a brand proposition offers is focus. VWs have come in a wide range of shapes and sizes over the last 40 years, but the core proposition for the brand since the 1960s has been 'reliability'. This core proposition brings integrity to the whole brand offering and a consistent platform on which to build more specific features and benefits. An effective employer brand proposition should play a similar role in bringing focus and consistency to the employee's experience of the organisation.

The first reference point for this proposition should be the organisation's corporate vision or mission. Do these statements of intent encapsulate a 'big idea' that can be translated into the employment context? By 'big idea' we do not mean a bigger market share or the greater enrichment of shareholders, we mean something of more universal value that the organisation believes it can bring to the world. In his book of the same title, Richard Jones described a 'big idea' as something that will: 'Create a special and palpable spirit within the business . . . [and] appeal equally to people inside and outside the organisation.'[2] Among the examples he gives are IKEA's 'Democratisation of design', Starbucks' 'Coffee as a cult' and Virgin's 'Iconoclasm'.

Microsoft provides a good example of translating this kind of 'big idea' into an employer brand proposition. Microsoft's big idea is 'Realising potential', with a unifying mission to 'work to help people and businesses throughout the world realise their full potential'. In turn, this has been translated into an employer brand proposition that focuses on creating 'an environment where great people can do their best work, and realise their potential'. It has also helped them to integrate their employer and customer brand communications which both share the tagline: 'Your potential. Our passion.'

If you do not feel that the corporate vision or mission provides an appropriate 'big idea' with which to align your proposition, the next place to look is the customer brand proposition. If the employer and customer brand name is the same, there is a clearly an advantage in trying to create a strong link. Take First Direct, for example. Its customer proposition states: 'The real difference about First Direct is simple. Most banks are about money. First Direct is about people.'[3] As they also say, it's a simple idea, but also 'revolutionary', in the context of banking services, and a big enough idea to translate directly into their proposition, which expresses what this focus on people means in the employment context: 'We're warm and witty. We're straightforward. We're understanding and responsive. We're unique.'

SouthWest Airlines provides a similarly good example of this alignment of the employer and customer brand proposition from the USA. In 1999 it translated its customer proposition, 'A symbol of freedom', into the employer brand proposition, 'Freedom begins with me'.[4] This proposition was not only used to emphasise the value that employees deliver to customers by giving them the freedom to fly, but also to reinforce the value to employees of the free flights, and wide range of other benefits offered by the company.

If you are struggling to make such a direct connection with the corporate vision and purpose or customer proposition, there are a number of other avenues that may provide you with a compelling and relevant hook. In most cases this involves building on one of the organisation's established (or potential) strengths, as illustrated by the following list of recruitment slogans taken from recruitment advertisements appearing in *The Times Top 100 Graduate Employers*[5]:

- Career opportunities (Morgan Stanley: *'Strides not steps'*)
- Personal growth (AstraZeneca: *'Space to grow'*)
- Freedom (Orange: *'Go where you want to go'*)
- Global reach (Baker & McKenzie: *'Expand your horizons'*)
- Challenge (Army: *'Be the best'* and P&G: *'A new challenge every day'*)

- Creativity (BAE systems: *'Platform for innovators'*)
- Cutting edge technology (Airbus: *'Setting the standards'*)
- Inherent value (GSK: *'Together we can make life better'*)
- Spirit (Diageo: *'If we could we'd bottle it'*)
- Confidence (Slaughter and May: *'Look forward in confidence'*)
- Intelligence (WPP: *'Ambidextrous brains required'*)
- Intrigue (MI5: *'For a life less ordinary'*)
- Sector appeal (Arcadia: *'Are you cut out for fashion?'*)
- The total package (JP Morgan: *'The 360° career'*)

While these are recruitment slogans rather than fully rounded propositions, they provide an indication of some of the positioning routes that your organisation may consider.

Before you finalise your employer brand proposition you should ask yourselves the following questions.

- Is it sufficiently aligned with the corporate and/or customer proposition?
- Is it credible?
- Would current employees recognise the underlying truth of the claim?
- Could you provide tangible evidence to substantiate the claim?
- Is it relevant and compelling?
- Does it strike the right emotional chord with both your internal and external target audiences?
- Does it differentiate you from your most immediate competitors?

If the answer is 'yes' to all of the above, then you are likely to have a winning proposition.

Values

Most organisations already have a set of values, if not several sets of values. It is not uncommon for corporate values to live alongside brand values, and in some cases several often competing sets of value-like descriptors. In one case we came across an organisation that presented eight 'cultural characteristics', eight 'core competencies', five 'organisational values' and four 'brand values'. We found out subsequently that they also had a dozen ethical principles, but presumably there wasn't room on the page to present them. Comprehensive, you may agree, but clear? There has definitely been a general tidying up and rationalisation of value statements over recent years. About five years ago I was involved in producing a new set of corporate brand guidelines for the BBC. When I first arrived there were 16 core values. After much soul searching this was whittled down to 11 brand values. There are now *six*. I seem to remember some scientific research that claimed that most people could hold no more than five separate thoughts in their heads at any one time. That feels about right, and the vast majority of value statements today list no more than five or six. The point is that not only do people have difficulty remembering more than a handful of value statements, but you can only describe a reasonably limited number of values as 'core'.

In the context of the employer brand the temptation to avoid is adding an additional set of values to those already in existence. In most cases, the main task is to ensure that the current values are made relevant and meaningful to employees. If the values were defined solely in the context of customers, you are likely to have to work harder at this than if the values are already corporate and organisational. If there are competing sets of values, the task is to simplify and rationalise. As mentioned in an earlier chapter, one way of doing this is to clarify the difference between generic organisational principles, and specific customer brand values. This simple act of repositioning often helps to differentiate between the different roles each set of statements play.

If the task is to create a new set of values or to refresh the old set of values, then we suggest that you try as hard as possible to keep it simple, and keep in mind both employees and customers. The rationale for this is that employees are far more likely to believe that the values are authentic and 'live the values' in their interactions with customers if these values are reflected in their own experience of the organisation. It's a very simple concept, and one that is often overlooked. People tend to treat others as they are treated themselves. If you look after your employees, they are far more likely to look after your customers.

First Direct again provides a good example of this approach. Their values are: Openness, Respect, Contribution, Responsive, Right first time and Kaizen (better and better). These are customer brand values, but they stress that they are also their employer brand values. They are designed to shape their employees' experience of First Direct as much as the customer experience. As their Commercial Director, Peter Simpson, commented: 'You can't pretend to be one style of brand to your consumers if you're a different style of brand to your people. It's the people who deliver your company interface; therefore the two have to be the same.'[6]

In defining your values you also need to be mindful of the real values that currently exist within the organisation (the brand reality). Stray too far in an overly aspirational direction, and the value statements will lack credibility. There is always a temptation for the leadership team to get together and dictate what they think the values should be. Unless the house is burning down, and a more dictatorial lead is expected, we would recommend a more democratic approach. The most successful value programmes that we have witnessed and been involved in have tapped into the inherent aspirations of employees. Most people want to work in a better organisation. Most people would prefer that organisation to be the one in which they currently work. Employees tend to have a good feel for what the organisation can be like at its best, and it is within this zone of reasonable stretch that we believe most value statements should be pitched.

It also helps to provide some differentiation. People in Business recently conducted some analysis into the value statements of the FTSE 100 companies. The top five most frequently stated values will come as little surprise. Of the 50 companies that publish their values on their websites, 38% stated 'integrity' as a core value, 26% 'teamwork', 24% 'innovation', 22% 'respect' and 18% 'performance'. These values represented the bedrock of corporate value statements, however, the tail of relatively unique statements was surprisingly long. Most of these top companies play relatively safe with the majority of their values, but generally have one or two that are truly differentiating – for example, BP's statement of 'green' as one of its four core values. Very few of these top companies have promoted environmental concern from the general ranks of CSR principles to front-ranking values. Likewise Compass Group's statement of 'diversity' as a core value was a relatively rare exception. If you choose 'creativity' (Cairn Energy), 'urgency' (GSK), 'straightforward' (BT) or 'decisiveness' (Cable & Wireless), you will be taking the path less trodden. Choose 'imagination' within this corporate community and you would be unique.

Personality

If values state what the organisation believes in, the employer brand personality describes how these beliefs tend to be expressed in terms of tone and style. To some extent the two concepts are closely intertwined; however, some important features of an organisation's personality tend to be missed if you just focus on values. The personality of an organisation generally shines through in its communication style. This will tell you whether the organisation is down to earth, serious, passionate, caring, off-beat, challenging, fun, the kind of adjectives you'd use to describe someone you know reasonably well. It helps to define your personality if you are striving to bring greater consistency to the overall tone and style of your communication. As with values, the customer brand proposition should be one of your first points of reference. If you are trying to communicate a certain kind of personality externally, it helps to ensure that this is carried through to your internal communications. Ideally, the external brand personality should already reflect the internal culture. If not, there may be some serious work to do to bring these two facets of your brand into closer alignment.

Customers have a very keen nose for the inauthentic, and they will notice just as fast as your employees if there is something phony in the personality you're trying to project if it's not deeply rooted in how the organisation feels. Take McDonald's, for example. There appears to be a huge gulf between the happy, smiley, family orientation of the external brand personality, the tired, McJob drudgery of its front-line employees and the faceless, corporate machine that appears to exist behind the façade. By its own recognition, McDonald's has lost its way over recent years, and refreshing the personality of the organisation to bring it more in line with the 'I'm lovin' it' ideal of the customer brand is as much on the agenda as salads and fresh fruit. In comparison, Virgin Atlantic is an example of an organisation whose youthful, vibrant, somewhat sexy brand personality feels true to the core. Their employees always seem to be genuinely upbeat. Their recruitment advertising, like their customer advertising, is quirky and fun. One of their most recent campaigns features real crew members portraying the 'Gods and Goddesses of Good Service'. This includes 'Gusto, the God of gentle breezes and youthful journeys', and 'Somnia, the Goddess of starry skies and splendid slumber'. This has not only proved highly successful in attracting new recruits, but also highly popular among the current cabin crew whose role in delivering a 'heavenly service' experience it clearly recognises and celebrates. As a final indication of this brand's integrity, I recently discovered that the internal team briefing process at Virgin Atlantic is called V.I.A.G.R.A. Enough said.

Benefits

In the employment context, benefits usually mean financial perks like a pension or a private health scheme. What we mean in the employer brand context is the wider range of functional and emotional benefits that people derive from their experience of work. Many of these, such as career opportunities and personal growth, we have already touched on in terms of the proposition statement. While the proposition statement should try to capture the most compelling advantage offered by the employer, the overall positioning statement should also list some of the other supporting benefits that characterise the complete employment offer. You should be able to derive a number of these from the current reality positioning. The task in defining your employer brand vision is to re-emphasise these strengths, address your weaknesses, and develop further qualities that will further increase your external appeal and drive higher levels of employee engagement. As we described in Chapter 8, correlation analysis should help you to identify the factors that most drive employee engagement and this should be combined with your insights into the factors driving attraction in the labour market.

Tesco provides a good example of an employer that has clarified and prioritised the benefits that most appear to drive commitment to the organisation. In Tesco's case these are defined as:

1. *Trust and respect* – The most important commitment driver for most employees is having a positive relationship with their workmates and manager.
2. *An interesting job* – The second most important commitment driver for many is the degree of interest they find in the jobs they perform.
3. *The opportunity to get on* – This relates to the opportunity to improve on their current pay package and benefits, and advance their career.

4. *A boss who supports me* – This relates to the general level of support people receive in terms of communication with their line manager, control over their workload, and opportunities for training and development.

Nationwide Building Society conducted a similar piece of research into the most important drivers of employee commitment that led it to define the following key benefits:

1. Fair and equitable pay, based on regular performance reviews.
2. Coaching and development, including a focus on leaders and managers as coaches and easy access to online advice, learning centres and career opportunities.
3. Effective resource management, reducing administration to create more time with customers, and avoiding people feeling under- or over-stretched.
4. Pride and belief in the values of the organisation.

Compass Group is not only the world's largest foodservice company, but also the world's ninth largest employer. Until recently Compass had largely grown through acquisition, with over 165 companies joining the Group within the last 13 years. Two years ago the company switched its focus to organic growth, and set its sights on becoming known as a great company, renowned as much for the quality of its people and service as it had been for its results – a self-styled journey from good to great. A key element of this has been the development of an employment brand for the Group, vital to attracting, developing and retaining the 'great' people the company needs to deliver its vision and continue to be successful. With over 400 000 employees distributed across 90 countries, this employer brand proposition needed to be both simple to understand and credible across a wide range of different businesses. The resulting proposition, arrived at through extensive research among its own employees, is called 'great people, real opportunities'. This was supported by eight 'real opportunities' reflecting the most important drivers of employee engagement identified from a global survey involving 290 000 of their 400 000 employees. These subcomponents of the overall proposition were defined as follows:

1. To have a great start.
2. To have work/life balance.

3. To learn and grow.
4. To be in the know.
5. To make a positive impact.
6. To be recognised.
7. To share rewards.
8. To share great ideas.

Each of these statements encapsulates a promise to deliver a positive employee experience in relation to such key elements of people management as induction, flexible working, learning and development, internal communication, recognition, reward and knowledge sharing.

Differentiators

Underline the features above that you believe will most differentiate the organisation from others in the future.

EMPLOYEE VALUE PROPOSITIONS

While the above elements define the overall positioning of the employer brand to all target groups, the question is how do you maintain employer brand consistency without limiting your flexibility to attract and retain different types of employee? This is clearly an important consideration for your employer brand strategy, because with many different types of employee to cater for (according to level, function, etc.) you will need to offer more than Vanilla to compete in the job market and to grow and keep the different kinds of people you need. These tailored 'packages' are generally described as Employee Value Propositions (or EVPs). The EVP is not just a tailored financial package, but a summary of the other specific benefits promised to different target groups.

For a great example of how this can work in practice, visit the Microsoft website, where you will find a separate section devoted to each major career segment.[7] You will note that they all reflect the underlying 'realise your potential' proposition, but tailor how this is expressed to each target group.

* **Technical EVP**: *Make a difference* – 'A career at Microsoft offers you the chance to be in the forefront of technological development, working with smart colleagues on meaningful projects. It's an opportunity to enjoy impact and ownership; your responsibilities have the potential to leave a lasting technological legacy.'

- **Marketing EVP**: *Your Impact Knows No Boundaries* – 'There's a certain satisfaction in knowing that your strategic marketing ideas help connect technology to millions of people around the world. In a marketing career at Microsoft, the possibilities of making an impact are limitless.'
- **Human Resources EVP**: *Fulfillment Is the Catalyst for Achievement* – 'It's an important mission bringing the right people in and taking good care of them. It plays a critical role in helping Microsoft generate technology that positively affects the lives of millions of people around the world. This mission is also your opportunity to discover just how far your abilities, ideas, and skills can advance your career. In Human Resources at Microsoft, your big ideas matter and we want to see them take you far.'

Reasons to Believe

The brand positioning model needs to be more than a briefing note for brand communication. It should also drive substantive change. An essential discipline in testing the validity of the model is to list each element in turn, and define the tangible reasons why employees and prospective candidates should believe them to be true. For the majority of the elements, this support should be firmly based on current activities, with a clear indication of what else the organisation plans to do to further support the brand promise. There is room for some more stretching claims, such as a major new focus on innovation, in an otherwise relatively uncreative organisation, but only if it is clear that this internal brand aspiration will be supported by a significant effort to make it real. We will touch on this subject in greater depth in Chapter 11.

SUMMARY

1. The purpose of brand positioning statements is to define what your brand currently stands for in the hearts and minds of your target audiences (the brand reality) and what you would like your brand to stand for in the future (the brand vision).
2. The nature and scope of your brand positioning models will depend on its relative standing within the wider organisation (monolithic, parent or subsidiary).

3. For brands that play a dual employee/customer facing role it is essential that the employer brand proposition and customer brand proposition are fully integrated. Ideally, they should both reflect a 'big idea' that can be expressed through every facet of the brand.

4. Your core employer brand proposition should provide a compelling, relevant and differentiating 'hook' for communication and shaping of the employment experience.

5. Just as different products and services exist within the portfolio of most customer-facing brands, employee value propositions represent the tailoring of specific employment 'packages' to different target groups of employees.

6. Brand positioning statements count for nothing unless they are founded on tangible and consistently experienced 'reasons to believe'.

Employer Brand Communication

While we have made it clear that there is far more to employer branding than 'sexing up' your recruitment materials or running a series of 'brand-wash' events, brand communication clearly plays a vital role in helping to improve people's understanding and perceptions of what the organisation has to offer.

IDENTITY

The first subject to tackle is employer brand identity. Do you need to create a new name for the employer brand? We suggest that the answer to this question in most cases should be 'no'. The integrity of the brand is vitally important to its credibility. While the brand may offer different propositions and benefits to a range of different internal and external audiences, there should always be a common core. By developing a separate employer brand name there is a danger of it being seen as an artificial gloss on the current reality, or a short-term initiative, rather than something of enduring meaning and substance.

There are some circumstances in which a new brand name may appear to represent the most workable solution. In 2003, Allied-Domecq launched an employer brand called 'Real Players'. The rationale for this new brand was that Allied-Domecq, with 500 subsidiaries in 50 countries, was essentially a holding company financial brand. While people in the head office work directly for Allied-Domecq, most employees around the world work for other organisational brands, such as Hiram Walker in the USA. The purpose of launching 'Real Players' was to develop 'a universal language to describe values and behaviour' and 'to create shared purpose'. While describing it as a global employer brand, 'Real Players' was more like an 'employee brand'. It described the employees who worked within the Allied-Domecq group rather than their ultimate employer. No one would ever say: 'I work for "Real Players".' From our perspective, by introducing this new brand name, the company missed the opportunity to give the real global employer brand 'Allied Domecq' fresh meaning and relevance. We would also suspect that most managers will have regarded it as a campaign initiative rather than something of lasting meaning within the business. Visiting the Allied Domecq website recently I noticed that the People section leads with: 'Our recent employee opinion survey speaks volumes about the pride our people take in their brands,' though clearly not 'Real Players'. There was no mention of it anywhere on the website.

An alternative route is to create a sub-brand, which can be used to identify 'employer brand' communication materials. Unilever use the sub-brand 'You', which unlike 'Real Players', always appears under the main corporate logo. This device has appeared in all of its recent recruitment advertising, and related internal briefing materials. This neat play on words provides a simple way of personalising the corporate, while retaining the integrity of the core employer brand, Unilever. The next step, as the Unilever employer brand team recognise, is to ensure that the meaning of the employer brand is more fully embedded internally.

While Unilever's simple and direct approach to sub-branding appears to have been effective, we would generally recommend caution in introducing any further branding elements that might detract from the more enduring core identity of the organisation. We believe this caution should also extend to 'branding' the internal launch.

INTERNAL LAUNCH

Once you have sharpened up your employer brand proposition there is always a great temptation to fast forward to an internal launch. The danger with most internal communication campaigns is that they tend to start with a bang, then fade away, to be superseded by the next campaign. Employees tend to be cynical about the latest 'big initiative' as they tend to have seen many such initiatives come and go without really changing very much. In large organisations there can be many internal initiatives running concurrently, each with its own call to action, launch pack and instruction guide. In many cases there is no obvious alignment between the initiatives, and sometimes apparent conflict. As a result, most employees within big organisations tend to be overwhelmed in terms of information and decidedly underwhelmed in terms of inspiration and engagement.

Brand engagement campaigns are particularly prone to cynicism. Whether they come in the form of internal 'living the brand' marketing exercises or CEO endorsed 'vision and values' or 'culture change', there is often a distinct sense of unreality about them. They tend to paint a compelling picture of the future, but seldom feel rooted in the current, day-to-day realities of the business. They promise much, but generally underdeliver. You will probably have come across the phrase 'sheep dip'; the sub-variant for brand engagement is 'the brandwash'.

Bearing all of this in mind, launching an employer brand can be fraught with difficulties unless it is carefully planned and executed. Having spent the last 10 years running numerous large-scale engagement campaigns, I think I can justifiably claim to have earned my bah, bah, black-belt in sheep dipping. The following represents my best advice in avoiding the pitfalls and launching something that will endure.

Our model for promoting brand engagement (Figure 10.1) involves three principal elements: think, feel and do. We believe that launch

Figure 10.1 The brand engagement model. *Source:* People in Business

campaigns need to address all three with equal rigour to achieve anything of lasting value.

RATIONAL UNDERSTANDING

For people to buy into the employer brand they first need to understand the context in which it is being introduced. Why is it being launched now? What will it help the business to do? And what's in it for them? The first two questions should be closely interlinked. In our experience, employer brands need a strong business context to justify a major launch. The most typical examples of this are:

1. A major external brand relaunch, in which case the role of the employer brand is to support the behaviour change necessary to deliver the new brand promise. As we have stated in previous chapters, people will be a lot more likely to play their part in shaping a new customer brand experience if they experience similar values and benefits themselves as employees.
2. A significant change in organisational strategy, restructuring, re-engineering, downsizing, right-sizing, centralising, decentralising, etc., in which case the role of the employer brand is to help to re-define the employees relationship with the new organisation.
3. A new corporate identity, in which case the role of the employer brand is to imbue the visual redesign with deeper organisational meaning and relevance.
4. A merger or acquisition, in which case the role of the employer brand is to help to establish a sense of shared purpose and identity.

Clearly, these contexts are not mutually exclusive, and often come bundled together in one major change project. The point is, they all represent moments of truth for the organisation, with a requirement to re-define the 'psychological contract' between the organisation and its employees. We would regard this as an ideal opportunity to launch the employer brand, as the role it plays in supporting the strategic objectives of the organisation can be made immediately clear.

In the absence of significant and tangible change, we would advise against a major launch to employees. We believe that a more appropriate approach in this context would be a more targeted management briefing and commitment to improving those aspects of the employment experience that support the underlying employer brand proposition. Typically this starts with a clearer recruitment advertising brief, though it could involve many other elements of the employer brand mix discussed in the next chapter. In the absence of a burning need to support a major change initiative, we suggest that this more incremental, activity-based approach is likely to win greater support than a stand-alone, big bang launch.

Whether you opt for a major launch, or take a more gradual approach to introducing your employer brand to employees, the clarity and focus of the communication is key. The overwhelming evidence from external brand research is to 'keep it simple'. Consumers receive thousands of brand messages each day, and advertisers need to keep their core messages simple and direct to cut through. While employees are sometimes regarded as a more captive audience, in reality they are just as likely to suffer from information overload. Employer brand messages therefore need to be equally simple and direct. Ensure that you are absolutely clear about the two to three core messages you want employees to consistently associate with the employer brand, and put 90% of your attention into getting these core messages across. This may mean sacrificing some of the more detailed information you would ultimately like to communicate to employees, but if you take the longer term view, as we will discuss shortly, it should be possible to build this up over time.

You not only need to be clear in your communication, you also need to ensure relevance, and this starts with the language you use. As some of our early research with the London Business School revealed, the use of brand language can be anathema to many employees. This is not just a question of being cynical about marketing; it is more a question of being cynical of jargon. Even in the context of a new customer brand positioning, employees do not need to be familiar with brand jargon to understand the importance of reputation or delivering value to customers. You would never use brand jargon in communicating the benefits of your brand to customers, so why use it with employees? While brand marketing tools are extremely useful in defining *how* communication with employees takes place, it is far more effective to frame *what* is communicated in terms that employees will more readily understand as relevant and meaningful to their everyday working lives. This 'plain speaking' approach also tends to focus the mind on the substance of the brand offering rather than the 'wrapping'. Calling a spade a spade means you need to make damn sure the spade is in good working order!

The clarity of the language you use becomes particularly important when you are dealing with large numbers of employees for whom English is a second language. Translating a core proposition into many different languages can result in a lack of consistency. It can also be very expensive. Where possible it appears that most global companies use English to communicate the core proposition, but ensure that the language remains clear and simple. This was one of the principal reasons for Compass Group choosing the phrase 'From Good to Great' in describing the objectives of their global HR strategy and new employer brand proposition. As Tracy Robbins, the group HR Director for leadership and development, who played a significant role in the programme, commented: 'The phrase "good to great" was effective because of its universality.' Apparently the only countries in which they needed to translate this core message were China (where 'great' means 'rich') and Spain, where 'great' does not convey the power of the meaning intended.

The second aspect of relevance that lies right at the heart of the employer brand concept is ensuring the relevance of the brand to the employment experience. Many 'living the brand' campaigns focus almost entirely on how the employee needs to behave to deliver the desired brand personality and value to the customer. This is, of course, relevant in terms of the commercial objectives of the company, but it fails to address the more direct benefits of the organisation's brand values to the employee. Employees are far more likely to accept the organisation's brand messages if they experience the worth of the values for themselves. Taking a selection of typical service brand messages to make the point, do the employees of the hotel chain that claims to be 'Always warm, always friendly' feel that way about their management team? Do the employees of a leading mobile phone company feel 'connected'? Does the technology company that offers its customers 'sense and simplicity' ensure that it delivers things in a user friendly format for its employees? I expect that in many cases this is a constant challenge, and that the proverb of the cobbler's children going without shoes captures the common experience within many organisations.

EMOTIONAL ENGAGEMENT

People may understand a message, but it makes little difference unless they care. It strikes me that the difference between a product and a brand is much like the difference between an indifferent employee and a fully engaged one. It's all about the extra meaning and value that positive emotions bring to the equation. When people are fully engaged they will go the extra mile, and in a highly competitive world, it's the extra mile that makes all the difference. While we have already addressed the general subject of employee engagement in the previous chapter, it takes on a more specific aspect when it comes to internal communication. How do you get people to engage with a new set of messages and ideas?

The first principle of active engagement is that it requires active leadership. There is nothing more engaging than personal contact with someone who is already highly engaged, particularly if that person has the power to shape the course of the organisation. It should be clearly evident from the beginning that earning the reputation for being an employer of choice, and delivering a consistently positive employee experience, needs to be a personal mission of the CEO, not just good housekeeping. In most of the positive examples we have encountered, this commitment is crystal clear. Sir Terry Leahy of Tesco, Tom Glocer of Reuters, Michael Bailey of Compass Group and Steve Ballmer of Microsoft are leading examples of leaders who have provided this kind of vocal, active and long-term commitment.

There is an enormous benefit to be derived from the CEO going on tour to carry the message directly to employees, as Chris Gent did soon after bringing together the disparate family of local brands under the Vodafone brand name. However, this can take a great deal of time and is often impractical. The common alternative is for the senior team to share these responsibilities, and host a series of events designed to launch the key messages, and brief people on the ensuing change plans. Where the organisation is large and widely dispersed, the role of the senior team is often to 'light the fire and fan the flames', by which we mean engage the next management layer or two down, and then support the enrolment of 'ambassadors' to carry the message out to the furthest reaches of the organisation. This can take an enormous logistical effort, and a fair degree of courage. I recall the nervous apprehension before embarking on a significant internal brand roll-out for Barclays in the late 1990s. We were due to brief the top 3000 managers on the bank's new brand positioning, running 17 events across four locations in the UK over a four-week period. The delegates arrived at 6 pm in the evening for an introductory presentation before dinner. This was followed by a full day's activities, finally closing at 5 pm. We then had an hour to turn around, including a final briefing session for the Barclays' ambassadors involved in facilitating the event, before beginning the process all over again with the next wave of delegates arriving at 6 pm. Even with carefully planning and a series of pilot sessions, this kind of intensive cascade always feels like a tough mountain to climb. However, what it does ensure is that people receive a consistent message and they receive it face to face from the leadership team.

A further benefit of this kind of event is that it helps to dramatise the key messages. As the 1960s media guru Marshall McLuan once said 'The medium is the message', by which he meant the channel through which something is delivered often communicates as much as the content of the message itself. In the context of an event, the fact that it is being staged outside the normal business premises, and delivered personally by a senior leader within the business, signals that the message is important. The fact that many otherwise separate groups of people have come together to participate in the event signals that it is a message designed to bring people together. In the Barclays case, these brand engagement sessions were one of the first initiatives to bring together people from both the retail bank and the business/corporate bank. These factors help to dramatise some of the underlying messages that the organisation wants to get across. The very act of 'staging' an event for a large group of people also helps to imbue the messages with drama. People on stages act differently to when they are in small briefing sessions. People within large groups also respond differently. It's the difference between watching football on the television and experiencing the match live in the stadium. There is a quantum leap in atmosphere (as long as the performance is up to scratch!).

Film can also deliver a more powerful effect on a big screen, and a well-constructed dramatisation of the brand messages on film can be highly engaging. From our experience the general quality of corporate videos has improved dramatically over the last decade, and many have been designed to deliver maximum impact on the big screen. The 'talking heads' formula, by which I mean senior managers providing context and pledging commitment to the cause on video, is really a small screen format. What has become far more common is for employees to be used in more dramatic situations to get the message across, and for the senior managers to ensure that they deliver their messages face to face (which communicates far more powerfully than any statements they may commit to video). The best recent example I have seen of this was not corporate at all, it was a video made by the west London Council of Ealing that delivers local government services to a population of 300 000 residents and 10 000 local businesses. In support of a major programme of internal transformation called 'Making a world of difference', it produced a 5-minute video which sought to communicate the essence of what they were trying to achieve to their 7500 employees. This was used in a wide-ranging programme of internal briefing and engagement events that have now touched the vast majority of their employees. Now you're probably thinking that a local government video is going to be pretty dry and imaginative. Well, think again. To dramatise the core proposition of 'Making a world of difference' they based the video on the story of 'It's a Wonderful Life'. If you haven't seen the film, it's an all-time classic. It features Jimmy Stewart as a well-meaning, regular guy who devotes his life to serving the local community as the manager of the local bank. Faced with almost certain bankruptcy, he contemplates suicide, but angelic intervention gives him an opportunity to return to his local town to see what it would have been like if he had never been born. During this return visit he begins to realise the true value of the many small acts of kindness that have characterised his life. I won't spoil the ending, suffice to say it makes for a compelling story. What Ealing did was to film different groups of employees telling the story to each other while going about their daily activities. What the film dramatised, in a gently humorous but also very moving way, was how the thousands of small daily activities carried out by the Council's employees contribute towards the community's collective quality of life. The film was both highly imaginative and down to earth. It highlighted Ealing's service proposition while, at the same time, celebrating the vital role of employees in contributing something of real value to people's lives. The next time you consider a 'talking heads' video to launch an internal brand message, think again about whether the level of creative imagination involved is going to do justice to the message you're trying to get across.

Even with the most inspirational of leaders, the most dramatic of venues and a brand video shot by Ridley Scott, you may still be lacking one vital ingredient in fully engaging your audience. Fortunately it is tends to be a rather less expensive ingredient. The most effective engagement tool is active audience participation and involvement. Probably the most successful brand vision event I was ever involved in organising did not take place at a swanky conference venue nor did it involve a long and rousing opening speech from the company President (though he was there). It took place in a large, empty warehouse. The first task of the day involved the 200 participants constructing and painting the conference set, and then planning and designing the agenda from scratch, in one hour. There's nothing like a challenge to get people engaged. The underlying message centred on the organisation setting out to achieve what appeared to be unachievable, together and fast. The senior team didn't have all the answers, but they were clear on the ambition to build one of the biggest brands in the UK. The set was built, the agenda was delivered and the organisation was Walkers Snack Foods.

While this kind of interactive 'event' tends to involve audiences of between 50 and 300 people, new technology has facilitated some interesting developments in mass participation events. When Reuters set out to win internal support for their Living FAST programme they leveraged their technical expertise to the full to involve over 15 000 employees in one interconnected, global, 24-hour event. To build interest prior to the event, this exercise also involved an online 'issues audit', which provided every employee with the opportunity to raise challenges that they felt needed to be addressed. These issues were then clustered into 23 challenges that were picked up by different teams around the world during the course of the main event. This helped to reinforce the point that the roll-out process was not just designed for the leadership team to broadcast their intent, but also to listen, share and respond to employees' concerns and suggested solutions. (See Reuters case study, Appendix 1, for more details.)

IBM's 'Jam Sessions' have been equally bold in scope. Described by one media commentator as 'the business world's Woodstock of online collaboration', IBM's first 'WorldJam' held in 2001, involved 52 000 employees in a 72-hour online conference to discuss 10 major cross-company issues. The event generated a significant number of new ideas and encouraged interaction across the company in a way that would have been impossible offline. This event has subsequently been followed up by a 'Management Jam' focusing on leadership issues and a 'Values Jam' seeking input on the relevance and vitality of the organisation's core principles.

Employee involvement need not require a major event. Some of the most powerful engagement techniques involve relatively simple exercises that can be conducted in relatively small briefing sessions. As any experienced facilitator will tell you, the trick in getting people to both think and engage is not to provide all the answers but to ask the right questions. As Nicholas Ind puts it in his useful guide to 'Living the Brand': 'The real challenge here is to change a manager's mindset away from an approach that focuses on selling an idea to others in the organisation to a more organic method, which following the planting of a seed of an idea, grows through the involvement and enthusiasm of others.'[1] The power of this approach was brought home to me during the process of conducting a long series of internal workshops introducing Unilever's new Code of Business Principles. While I believe, as you will gather from the Ealing example, that well-constructed brand stories can help to illustrate key messages, the most engaging approach is to present open-ended scenarios. We used both in communicating Unilever's core principles, but time and again, the more powerful of the two approaches in delivering engagement and emotional buy-in were the scenarios. The following insert provides an example of one of the scenarios we used to explore the principles of 'business integrity' and 'fair competition'.

Scenario – Taking a Lead

- *The marketing director of Avanta is approached by a talented but dissatisfied young brand manager from its main competitor Besto.*
- *Agreeing to an interview, the marketing director is interested to discover that Besto is planning a major new relaunch.*
- *He asks his team to keep an eye out for any further information that might indicate when the launch is due.*
- *An eager sales representative manages to uncover Besto's media schedule, carelessly left on a trade customer's desk.*

- *The marketing director pre-empts the Besto relaunch with a major price promotion and significantly spoils its impact.*
- *Should the marketing director be congratulated?*

The underlying point of these scenaria was to demonstrate that organisational values and principles are seldom black and white. While they are generally easy to understand at face value, they are often far harder to apply in the real world. On the page, values and principles appear obvious and absolute, but the real world is full of conflicting pressures, trade-offs and compromises that can make 'values' appear unrealistic (and too often irrelevant). It would be inadvisable, if not impossible, to create a rule book covering every conceivable situation in which a value or principle may need to be applied, so you have to communicate the spirit and essence of the value, and rely on people to make active judgements. By providing people with true to life dilemmas, you can help them to explore and interrogate the values for themselves, and in doing so, shift the context of the communication from receiving instruction, to taking personal ownership.

In the above example, should the marketing director have agreed to the interview if there was no suitable vacancy available? At what point between an innocent slip of the tongue and aggressive interrogation would the principle of integrity have been betrayed in discovering Besto's relaunch? Should the marketing director have shared this knowledge? Should the marketing director have been more specific in describing what he meant by 'to keep an eye out'? At what point between taking note of a poster on the wall through to uncovering a partially obscured document on the customer's desk would business integrity have been compromised? If the document had been 'uncovered' from someone's private desk, should the information have been acted on? After prompting discussion of these questions with the group, some general guidelines were provided on the definition of confidential material, the difference between private and public domain and the legal interpretation of soliciting for trade secrets. However, without any prompting the crux of most discussions focused not on the legal constraints to action, but the 'real' meaning and value of business integrity in the pressurised commercial world of day-to-day business. To give an indication of the level of engagement that this scenario-based approach achieved, the senior team of the Latin American

Business Group set aside two hours to cover what clearly appeared to them at first a cut and dry subject. The workshop lasted six hours, into the evening. They spent over an hour on the single scenario featured above.

EMPLOYEE COMMITMENT AND BEHAVIOUR CHANGE

There is a simple, well-known phrase that every business leader should take to heart in making internal brand promises: 'Actions speak louder than words.' From our perspective there is one very important difference between emotional engagement and commitment in the context of internal communication. Short term engagement can be bought with brand promises, but longer term commitment and behaviour change can only be earned by ensuring that those promises are substantiated.

Substantiating employer brand promises is much harder graft than making them. It sometimes appears that senior management teams think that the job is done when the brand message has been delivered and received, as though the organisation will suddenly transform itself having seen the light. But people will only believe the brand messages, and begin to change their behaviours if they begin to see tangible evidence from the top that the brand proposition and values are being hard wired into the fabric of the organisation, changing the way in which processes are run and important decisions are taken.

When Greg Dyke was Director General of the BBC he initiated a major programme of culture change called *Making it Happen*. This was supported by a restatement of the BBC's core values and a well coordinated series of internal events, including 'Just Imagine' and 'The Big Conversation'. These mass participation exercises shared much in common with the Reuters' June 11 event and IBM's 'Jam Sessions' described earlier. While extremely successful in promoting employee engagement, Greg Dyke believes the most powerful 'moments of truth' for the change programme were connected to actions not words. When I saw him speak on the subject at the Work Foundation in 2004, he mentioned two actions among many that he claimed reinforced commitment to the change programme more than anything else. The first was moving the BBC News from 9 pm to 10 pm. This may not appear to be much of a change, but the 9 o'clock News had been a central feature of the BBC's schedule for decades. Previously it was felt it would have taken 12 months of consultation and study papers to even begin to consider such a move. Within the new regime it was agreed and executed within two weeks, and reinforced the message that the BBC could be both decisive and dynamic. The second symbolic action was more humdrum in some respects, but nevertheless felt to have been equally significant. The BBC's White City office was a fairly ugly building with only one really attractive feature, the central atrium. The problem was that employees had been disallowed from using the atrium for the last 14 years, though nobody seemed to understand why. The reason, it turned out, was Health & Safety. The atrium needed a wheelchair ramp and second fire exit, but previous attempts to fix the problem had apparently proved 'too difficult', and were abandoned. While only a minor aspect of the overall change programme, fixing this problem and the opening up of the atrium to staff proved immensely symbolic. As Greg Dyke commented in his book *Inside Story*:

> The opening up of the White City atrium became an incredibly important story around the BBC. It symbolised what 'Making it Happen' was trying to do and helped convince people things could be changed. It showed the staff that the Director General was on their side in attacking the mind-numbing negativity of the BBC bureaucracy. It also told the jobsworth bureaucrats that we were after them.[2]

From such actions are employer brand reputations transformed, though whether this battle was ultimately successful at the BBC is doubtful.

In the next chapter, on brand management, we consider this kind of substantiation in terms of the employer brand 'mix'. The concept of the mix in marketing refers to the complete range of elements that shape the brand experience. They are sometimes called the 'touch-points', which is another way of describing how people's perceptions are derived from hundreds of different meetings with the brand. In the context of the employer brand there is perhaps more control over the communication touch-points, but there are also far more experiential touch-points than for your average customer brand.

Brand trust is generally based on brand consistency. Substantiation of the brand promises plays a key role in this, but it is also important to keep the brand message consistent. There is a tendency for internal programmes of brand engagement to be treated as a discrete stream of communication, unconnected to other subjects and sources of management information. If you take an employer brand perspective this does not hold up to close inspection. From the employee's perspective, all your internal communication has the potential to reinforce or undermine how people feel about the company. This means that you are unlikely to build trust and credibility in your employer brand unless you deliver a degree of consistency across all of your communications.

Vodafone provide a very good example of this. Their core values are: 'passion for our people', 'passion for our customers', 'passion for performance', and 'passion for the world around us'. They have consistently used these core values to frame a multiplicity of internal initiatives that have helped both to reinforce their saliency and substantiate them over time.

Another key area of focus is the consistency between internal and external communications. Don't forget that your external communication (including both recruitment and consumer advertising) can also send powerful messages to your employees about the kind of company you run, or claim to be running. You need to make sure your employees feel that these external promises are credible before you over-promise to customers or new recruits. Failing to consider the employee perspective, as in the Sainsbury's case (page 10) can be disastrous. On the other hand, closely involving your employees in the development of an external advertising campaign, as the Halifax have proved, can be an all-round winner. The Halifax conducted an internal competition involving over a thousand employee auditions in eight regional casting sessions to choose the new face of the bank. The resultant winner 'Howard' has subsequently proved to be immensely popular with customers and employees alike.

The final point on consistent communication is maintaining continuity over time. How do you continue to reinforce the same underlying messages while keeping it relevant and fresh? This is a major issue within brand management on which we have already commented in Chapter 6. Brand communication requires constant creative attention to find new ways of dramatising brand messages. This should not mean changing the core messages, but finding fresh ways of expressing them and building the story. Just consider some of the longest running UK advertising campaigns. Stella's 'Reassuringly Expensive' campaign has been running for over a decade, but still manages to create impact with each new execution. It's like the difference between launching a movie and launching a TV series. If you launch your employer brand as if it's a movie, with lots of fanfare and a big event, it can seem as if all the excitement is over once you leave. 'Well I've seen that movie what's next?' If you think of it more like a TV series, the dynamics are different. You establish the dramatic context, introduce the key characters, develop some interest and then you build.

The communications campaign that Nationwide Building Society used to support the introduction and embedding of its PRIDE values, provides a good example of this approach. The original launch in 2002 introduced all five values:

> **P**ut members first (Building Society's refer to their customers as 'members')
> **R**ise to the challenge
> **I**nspire confidence
> **D**eliver best value
> **E**xceed expectations

Subsequent to this the plan has been to keep all five values in mind but to highlight a different value each year. In 2003 the emphasis was placed on 'Inspiring confidence' in support of a focus on leadership behaviours. In 2004 the emphasis was placed on 'Delivering best value', supported with a challenge issued to the organisation to drive for greater efficiency. This has enabled Nationwide to maintain the relevance of the values without repeating the same story year on year.

SUMMARY

1. Communication plays a vital role in shaping people's understanding and perceptions of the employer brand.
2. In communicating the employer brand it is generally counterproductive to introduce additional branding elements that may detract from the more enduring core visual identity of the organisation.
3. We suggest that employer brand engagement campaigns should only be launched in association with other substantive changes

within the organisation or repositioning of the external corporate or customer brand.

4. To promote internal commitment to your employer brand it is important to establish both a strong rationale and appeal to the emotions of your employees.

5. Applying brand thinking and marketing tools to people management does not mean that you need to use brand jargon in your communication. It's no more relevant to your employees than your customers. You should focus on the benefits, not the underlying methodology.

6. Avoid the temptation to over-claim for dramatic effect. To ensure that your communication is credible, it's better to focus on what is already on offer, or soon to be available, rather than focus on a utopian vision that feels far removed from current reality.

7. Don't forget that your external communication (including both recruitment and consumer advertising) can also send powerful messages to your employees about the kind of company you are, or claim to be. Make sure your employees feel that external brand communication is credible before you over-promise to customers or new recruits.

8. Take the long-term view and be careful not to position employer branding as a campaign initiative. You know you wouldn't succeed in the marketplace by treating your external brand communication as a short-term initiative. By the same standards, you shouldn't expect to succeed in building a strong employer brand by putting all your emphasis on a big bang launch and then neglecting to follow through.

9. Recognise that from the employees' perspective, all your internal communication has the potential to reinforce or undermine how people feel about the company. You are unlikely to build trust and credibility in your employer brand unless you deliver a degree of consistency across all of your communications.

10. Don't' forget the 'body language' of the organisation. People pay far more attention to what is done than what is said. Look for ways of symbolising your intent through tangible actions, including attention to managers who feel that, as successful business 'operators', they are exempt from the brand values.

Employer Brand Management

11

It is one thing to establish the nature of your employer brand – what it is and what it needs to be to achieve your business objectives – but it is quite another to ensure that it is managed with the same care and coherence as you would a customer brand. If you fail to put in place the management systems and the senior management support for them, then the whole employer brand initiative may wither and result in nothing more than some tinkering with recruitment advertising.

A good example of the application of these skills can be found at Orange, where David Roberts (employment brand and communications manager), while an HR staff member, sits alongside Orange's marketing and advertising team. His job is to make sure that the people aspects of the Orange brand are correctly managed in the £50 million that Orange spends a year in the UK and, similarly, to ensure that consumer-facing work fits with the reality of the employment experience. Orange uses their employer brand to drive the market understanding of themselves as employers and to make sure that their communications in this field are consistent and compelling. They regard the Orange employer brand as an internal catalyst to drive initiatives that will ensure that Orange is a great place to work. They realise of course that it is much more than communications and they are using the Orange employer brand to drive the internal change they need to ensure that every relevant aspect of the employment experience 'does what it says on the tin'.

To this end there are four significant roles that must be coordinated within Orange HR. These are the head of physical environment, the head of employment and engagement (covering diversity, private surveys, etc.), the head of compensation and benefit and the head of HR business delivery, which provides all Orange businesses with the traditional HR services they need. The aim for this is to ensure that the Orange employer brand is realistic, desirable and unique and is the result of extensive internal and external research and the necessary internal change relationships that it has prompted.

An interesting hurdle that Orange employer brand management has to overcome is what they call Orange Shock. That is the term they use for potential disconnect that can exist between the young funky style of Orange in the marketplace and the detailed processes, heavy demands and serious commitment that the now vast organisation regards as essential. While David Roberts reports to the Head of Resources, his ultimate bosses are the Vice President for HR and the Vice President for Marketing and Branding. It is a good example of employer brand coherence.

Another example is PepsiCo UK, for years regarded as a top HR house, where the PepsiCo 'Umbrella' delivers a common purpose, a common identity and common values across the HR processes in businesses as varied as Walkers Crisps, Tropicana, Quaker and Pepsi itself. Camille Burrows is organisational and management development director for PepsiCo UK and when Simon Barrow first heard her speak at an employer brand event he was struck by the thought that she could just as easily be a marketing executive. Interestingly, before her HR work she started business life in a recruitment company and one thing recruitment people have to possess is a sense of opportunity and service delivery which makes them good salespeople. HR and employer brand management demand much broader skills, but this early experience definitely helps. Like Orange, PepsiCo UK have done their homework on people's motivations and commitment to the company. PepsiCo is an organisation in which, however well you have done, there will always be a greater goal and over time these seemingly endless 'false summits' have become a significant motivational issue. In response they have highlighted the need for stronger management recognition of the efforts made by individuals within a very demanding company. This PepsiCo research has not led to significant change in organisational development or compensation and benefits, but it has resulted in changes to people's attitudes and behaviours. This could only have been achieved with the full and proactive commitment of Martin Glenn, the president of PepsiCo UK, who some years earlier had commissioned me to conduct the first ever employer brand project for Walkers Snack Foods.

What particularly struck us about PepsiCo is that given the long-standing commitment to people processes from the top, the company does not seem to have any of the historic baggage of the Human Resources function. They were totally at one with the objectives and strategy of the business. Nevertheless, Camille's message for employer brand managers is 'you have to be brave enough to state what is right and stick to your guns'.

While there are a growing handful of employer brand manager job titles, it is our view that any good HR function with strong senior management involvement and support is perfectly capable of managing the employer brand. The specific title can help when, as in Sainsbury's case, there was a need to demonstrate that the coherence of brand management was a serious part of the organisation's intent. The term 'brand management' does communicate joined-up-ness, and that is the heart of this approach.

To help both in assessing your current employer brand reality, and planning how to deliver the employer brand proposition you desire going forwards, we have developed a list of 12 key dimensions which we refer to as the employer brand mix (Figure 11.1). We divide the 12 areas into two broad groups, the first relating to wider organisational context and policy and the second local context and practice. Each of these elements represents key 'touchpoints' for the employer brand.

BIG PICTURE: POLICY

External Reputation

There is often a close relationship between the employer brand image of a company and the reputation of its goods and services. It is generally assumed that an organisation that is capable of delivering a good external brand experience is also likely to be a good quality employer. The same can be said of companies that are known to be financially successful. Employees are understandably proud of working for organisations that are well known and well spoken of externally. It provides people with

Figure 11.1 The employer brand mix. *Source:* PiB

recognisable status (particularly on the CV) and a positive image that they will be more likely to advocate and live up to in their interactions with external parties.

It is always worth bearing in mind that employees will probably pay as much, if not more attention to your external marketing than your target customers. If handled well this can provide your organisation with a boost to employee engagement in addition to any further benefits you derive from improving your external brand image and driving sales. In this context, you should make sure your employees are well briefed on any high-profile marketing activities. Employees should understand what, if anything, is expected of them to support new promises or claims. If, as is increasingly common, your advertising incorporates 'employees' (actors or otherwise), you should make sure that this representation is well researched internally as well as externally. Are they credible role models, or merely dancing to the tune of the advertising message? In the Sainsbury's example discussed in Chapter 1, the lack of respect shown to the employee featured in the John Cleese advert was a major cause of employee disaffection. Likewise, employees can also feel disaffected by promises they know will be difficult to fulfil. A recent campaign run by the oil company Total featured a perfect employee called Steve who spends his whole time running around the forecourt helping customers with heavy loads, childcare, and car maintenance, with the tagline: 'You'll find people like Steve at all of our service stations.' Apart from being less than totally believable to customers, this kind of advertising can put an immense strain on employees. Unless it is well backed by training and additional support, it is far more likely to undermine their image of the organisation than enhance it.

Negative external coverage should also be well briefed internally as employees will often be asked their opinion. Employees are likely to be even more disaffected by bad news if they feel they know less than the newspapers. It is the natural tendency of most employees to defend their organisations, but they need the information to do so. Journalists will typically take the most negative view of circumstances. It is therefore important to make sure that employees are well briefed on the wider picture, including full and open recognition of any mistakes that have been made, so that they are in a strong position to respond to these 'moments of truth'.

Just as an effective product or service brand manager has a role to play in championing the customer's viewpoint, the role of employer brand management is to ensure that the employee's viewpoint is always taken into consideration in the development of external corporate or marketing communication.

Internal Communication

As we made clear in Chapter 10, all internal communication should be regarded as employer brand communication, as every piece of communication says something about the organisation. While a number of leading companies are beginning to coordinate their internal communication more effectively, it is still more typical for different functions and divisions to 'do their own thing'. From the employees' perspective this is likely to lead to perceptions of information overload and incoherence.

The role of brand management is to champion a more coherent and employee-centric view of internal communication. This involves a degree of 'air traffic control' to ensure that major communication efforts don't all try to land at the same time. It also involves a smarter approach to content management. Are the most significant corporate messages being consistently reinforced? Does the style of communication consistently support the desired values and personality of the organisation? Is there sufficient feedback and monitoring to ensure that the desired messages are getting through?

Senior Leadership

Of all the potential sources of communication, the leadership team has one of the most critical roles to play in both reinforcing the credibility and conveying the 'spirit' of the employer brand. Effective leadership is also one of the most powerful drivers of employee engagement. This has been corroborated by many benchmark studies, particularly ISR's three-year global employee engagement study published in 2002, which identified 'quality of leadership' as the foremost driver of employee commitment.[1] This does not necessarily mean that leaders need to spend all their time directly talking about the employment proposition, but it should inform the style in which they communicate, and how they structure their messages to reinforce the desired relationship between the organisation and its employees. The way in which the organisation's leaders behave will be equally important. The majority of employees have very well-honed bullshit detectors, and will spot the merest hint of false sentiment or management cliché if what is said deviates from the reality of their observations. When Greg Dyke starting sending e-mails to all employees with the sign-off 'Yours Greg', it signalled a more direct and personal style of leadership at the BBC. However, the symbolism of this gesture only gained credibility when it was noticed that his behaviour followed suit, such as taking his place in the lunch queue in the staff canteen (a noticeable departure from previous Director Generals of the BBC). The leadership team, particularly the CEO, has a significant role to play in not only communicating the proposition but also embodying the employer brand and its associated values in everything they say and do.

The role of employer brand management in relation to the senior leadership team is to ensure that they are constantly made aware of the impact of both their words and actions in shaping employees' perceptions of the organisation.

Values and Corporate Social Responsibility

Following the growing interest in CSR over recent years, there have been numerous studies into the effects of good practice in this area on employee engagement and commitment. When the Work Foundation and the Future Foundation conducted a study to examine the impact of CSR on the employer brand they reported that 20% of employees found employers with a positive socially responsible image more attractive.[2] They also noted a strong positive correlation between companies that are seen to take their responsibilities towards society seriously and those seen as a good employer to work for. In a similar study conducted by the Corporate Citizenship Company it was concluded that community involvement improves employee morale, motivation and the propensity of people to recommend their company to others.[3]

Two of the most important employee-related aspects of corporate responsibility are diversity and work–life balance. The diversity agenda of most leading organisations now extends well beyond 'equal opportunities'. It has begun to encompass a more far-reaching respect for individual differences in all their forms. Vodafone's statement of diversity policy is typical of this more positive attitude to diversity in claiming:

> We believe that diversity is a key driver of creativity, leadership and innovation . . . We are seeking to build a culture that respects the value of differences among us and encourages individuals to contribute their best within an environment that is inclusive, open, flexible and fair.[4]

Likewise, Unilever states:

> Diversity at Unilever means more than physical diversity – gender, nationality, style, race and creed. It's about us – creating an environment that inspires different individuals to contribute in their own different ways within a framework of shared values and goals.
>
> We strongly believe in creating an environment which fosters creativity and engenders powerful team commitment – an environment where differences are valued and where people can fully realise their true potential.[5]

In many respects, a commitment to work–life balance represents a natural extension of this philosophy, in that it encourages people to find a balance in their lives which allows them to perform at their best. In Chapter 3 we made reference to the negative effects of stress on many people's working lives, and this is one of the principal ways that organisations are beginning to address this issue. Leading commentators have noted that, work–life balance is fast becoming a highly significant component in becoming an 'employer of choice'. As Mike Johnson puts it in his book *The New Rules of Engagement*:

People – your employees – have come up with a different way of looking at it. It's called life–work balance. Life first, work later. And this is what is going to drive the new social contract between employer and employee.[6]

In this context, an organisation's CSR activities should be regarded as an important element within the employer brand mix, and not simply an exercise in 'doing the right thing' or bolstering the external corporate reputation.

Internal Measurement Systems

Our research into organisations with strong employer brands has repeatedly reinforced our belief in the maxim 'what gets measured gets done'. At the Nationwide Building Society, where levels of employee satisfaction and engagement in their annual 'Viewpoint' survey have been improving consistently for some years, the CEO Philip Williamson has made a habit of taking a direct interest in low- and high-scoring branches. This has made a significant impact on both raising the floor and the ceiling of people management performance. The transparent approach they take to their 360-degree evaluations has also been recognised as a significant spur to self improvement. We discovered a similar picture at Tesco where the local version of their balanced scorecard (the Steering Wheel) is regularly posted on the staff notice board. In both cases employees are assured that the company takes its proposition to employees seriously enough to measure it, publicise it and act on the results.

Service Support

The quality of the service support that employees receive internally – either when they need something urgently to satisfy a customer, or when they need help in responding to something more personal – represents a critical moment of truth for the employer brand. In organisations where the employee is principally regarded as either a worker drone or channel for getting the brand to market, the emphasis tends to be placed on schooling employees on what they are expected to deliver for the customer. This can provide a clear sense of alignment and customer focus, but there is a natural tendency for employees to question the authenticity of the brand and its supposed values if it doesn't resonate with their own experience of the organisation. I recall one employee from a heavily advertised service brand commenting:

> They are expecting us to be fast and efficient in terms of what we deliver to customers but where is the speed and efficiency when it comes to things that we want as employees? How can they expect us to be responsive to customers, when they are totally unresponsive to us?

This is one of the more difficult areas for employer brand management to address since it cuts across functional divides, and is often deeply rooted in the current culture of the organisation. Nevertheless, poor performance in this area can totally undermine the organisation's efforts to promote brand engagement. No amount of internal communication on the brand or customer focus will make up for the disengagement that can result from employees feeling devalued by their own experience of work.

LOCAL PICTURE: PRACTICE

Recruitment and Induction

Recruitment is seldom regarded as a transaction by new employees, but it often appears to be treated that way by employers. As we suggested in Chapter 9, brand managers tend to focus on the process of building a lasting brand relationship rather than simply signing up new customers, and they are aware that a customer's first experience of a brand represents a vital stage in creating a positive and enduring connection. How often can this be said of the recruitment and induction process? It tends to be well stage managed for graduates and senior recruits, but what about everyone else?

The recruitment process is also increasingly being tailored to identify the types of people who will have a natural affinity with the organisation's brand values. For example, the recruitment process Lego developed with Kaisen started with a web questionnaire that quickly identified and screened out people who did not have the right 'fit' for the job and the Lego brand.[7] For example, in subsequent Face to Face interviews, when asked to describe a customer, naturally empathetic candidates – those with a better fit to the brand – tended to talk about the customer's feelings and emotions, while less well-suited individuals just gave hard facts.

In terms of current employer brand practice most of the emphasis tends to be on recruitment, but from a brand management standpoint the induction process is equally important. This represents a golden opportunity to dramatise the character of the organisation, what it expects of its people, and what in turn the individual employee can expect from the organisation. It's an opportunity for which any passionate marketer would pay a large premium if it concerned a potentially valuable customer, but in actual internal practice it too often appears to be squandered.

Team Management

In the many recent studies that have explored employee engagement, the behaviour of local management is generally recognised as a vital success factor. In the engagement study conducted by IES the strongest driver of all was 'a sense of feeling valued and involved' and the quality of the employee's immediate management was identified as critical factor in bringing this about.[8] This echoed previous research conducted by ISR which listed the people management skills of an employee's immediate manager/supervisor, and an employee's feeling of empowerment to carry out work effectively as two of the most important drivers of employee commitment.[1] In *The War for Talent* study conducted among middle and senior managers, Michaels et al. found a similar pattern of response.[9] While they noted that different people prefer different kinds of corporate culture, they also found that nearly all managers look for 'an open, trusting environment'. This was particularly noticeable among younger managers (Generation X), who rated a 'good relationship with my boss' as one of the most important elements in driving their career decisions. On a more negative note, many other studies have continued to reinforce the observation that people 'join an organisation, but they leave their boss'.

From a brand management perspective, the day-to-day quality of local management plays just as important a role in shaping the employer brand experience, as the front-line customer representative plays in shaping the external brand experience (and, as we have sought to demonstrate, the two are intimately linked). This demands an involvement in leadership development and training. Does it support the behaviour required to deliver the employer brand proposition and high levels of employee engagement? If not, this will represent a major weakness in the long-term credibility and sustainability of the employer brand.

Performance Appraisal

One of the regular features we encountered in researching successful employer brands was the extent to which the core values of the organisation were embedded in the performance management process. At both Reuters and Nationwide we found that this was regarded as one of the most important factors in grounding the values in people's everyday behaviours. As John Reid-Dodick of Reuters observed, when you have spent several days evaluating people in terms of value-based behaviours, and been evaluated yourself in terms of your own performance in practising the values, then you begin to develop a much deeper sense of what those values mean in everyday practical terms.

Whether this occurs successfully depends of course on the quality of the process, and how rigorously it is applied at a local level. Are people clear about what is expected of them and how they will be judged? Is the appraisal properly prepared for by both appraiser and employee? Are people prepared to deal with poor performance?

In terms of clarity, we regard the guidance provided by Greggs plc, a leading UK retailer specialising in sandwiches, savouries and other bakery products, as exemplary (Appendix 3).

Learning and Development

Learning and development represent vital components of the employer brand offering. They influence both the organisation's general attractiveness to new recruits and its ongoing ability to maintain high levels of employee engagement.

In ISR's global commitment study (2002) 'development opportunities' were identified as the second most important driver of employee commitment, only marginally behind the leading factor 'quality of leadership'.[1] In ISR's more recent global study (2004) they identified career development as a cornerstone of employee engagement in nearly all of the 10 countries they studied.[10] Likewise, in the IES study on employee engagement (2004), training and development was rated as the most important influence on whether employees felt valued, involved and engaged.[8]

When Marks & Spencer researched its employer brand it noticed an interesting pattern in the data. People who had received training within the last six months were 19% more satisfied than those who had not received training. One of the most interesting aspects of this study was that recent training also appeared to deliver a 'halo effect'. Employees who had received training within the last six months were generally more satisfied with all aspects of the employer brand, not just development.

While research findings are consistent in identifying the importance of training and career development to employee engagement and the strength of the employer brand, there is just as much evidence to suggest that most employees feel that their employers could do a great deal more to improve their offering in this area.

In 1999, a global study conducted by the Career Innovation Research Group among over 1000 young professionals concluded that: 'These people have an overwhelming desire for personal and career development – for a "development contract" (to match the "performance contract") – yet their experience rarely matches their expectations.'[11] A more recent study by TNS suggests that little has changed over the last five years. They found that from the employees' perspective, 70% of US companies are failing to deliver sufficient opportunities to learn, grow and develop.[12] Our experience suggests that the situation in the UK will probably be similar despite the continued efforts of such organisations as Investors in People to raise the profile of training and development as a key performance-enhancing investment. Since this aspect of the employer brand mix appears to be generally weak, developing a more robust 'development contract' represents a significant opportunity for organisations to both differentiate their employer brand and drive higher levels of employee engagement.

Development does not, of course, stop with the exit from the company. We believe that a key question for anyone considering joining an organisation is to ask about the success of people who have left the company and moved on. Alumni are often the first port of call for people checking out your organization, and throughout their careers they will be talking about their time with you. Yet few employers regularly keep in touch with their alumni and many have only the most rudimentary processes for managing any kind of ongoing relationship. Try calling a switchboard and asking for someone who has moved on. More likely than not you will be told ominously that so and so is 'no longer with the company'. There is often also a tone of voice that implies that something has gone wrong. Our own view is that if an organisation cannot list the names of people who have gone on to great things then it is likely to reflect badly on the employer brand.

Reward and Recognition

As the authors of *The War for Talent* pointed out: 'While it takes more than money to build a winning EVP [Employee Value Proposition], if you don't stay competitive with the market price for the best managerial talent, you'll have a hard time.'[9] Just as the pricing of your services to customers requires constant attention and updating, the financial dimension of the employment package is always going to provide a baseline for the brand.

While reward is a major symbol of recognition it is only one of many. Survey after survey reveals that *recognition* is one of the most critical factors in employee motivation. Feeling valued (particularly for discretionary effort) is a critical factor in employee engagement, and recognition. Whether through prize giving or incentive schemes, or a general management tendency to offer praise for work well done, recognition is one of the simplest and most direct ways of demonstrating that people matter.

For Compass Group, recognition was identified as one of the most powerful drivers of employee engagement in their global employee survey, and they found a creative way of incorporating this into their employer brand roll-out by featuring professionally shot portraits of employees who had 'gone the extra mile' in their internal and external (recruitment) campaign materials. We hope that, by featuring a number of these portraits on the front cover of this book, we have also played a small part of our own in contributing to this recognition.

Working Environment

In a discussion with a communications manager from BT we were interested, though not surprised, to discover that the quality of people's working environment appeared to be a significant factor in determining how they responded to BT's recent values programme. Employees working in modern, well-furbished offices tended to be far more positive than those working in some of their older, less well-appointed sites. There were undoubtedly other contributory factors in this case, but our general experience suggests that people's working environment represents an important manifestation of the employer brand. It still appears that many organisations pay little attention to the working environment over and above the basic logistical and HSE necessities. In comparison, leading employer brands like Microsoft, Vodafone, Reuters and Hiscox go to great efforts to shape the office environment to reflect the core values and personality of the organisation. In Microsoft's case, this meant managing the wall space in public areas as carefully as they would high-profile external poster sites. For Vodafone it meant designing their new headquarters campus in Newbury with two of its core values '*Passion for our people*' and '*Passion for the world around us*' very much in mind.[13]

From our perspective, the 12 items shown in Figure 11.1 and discussed above are the most important elements to be considered within the employer brand "mix", but it is far from an exhaustive list. In addition to ensuring that the total mix is consistent with your overall employer brand proposition and values, the mix can also play an important role in differentiating yourselves from your competition. Just like the dimensions of a consumer product or service, each organisation must determine the elements that are going to help its employment experience to really stand out for the people it most needs to recruit and retain.

THE KEY RESPONSIBILITIES OF EMPLOYER BRAND MANAGEMENT

From our perspective there are five main roles to be performed by the person or people tasked with developing the employer brand strategy and ensuring its effective ongoing management.

- Establishing the nature of the employer brand required by the organisation to achieve its business objectives.
- Crafting an effective employer brand positioning and winning senior management involvement and approval for the resources and cultural changes that are necessary to make it a reality.

- Managing the communications necessary to reach the target audiences internally and externally.
- Developing a good working relationship with the many different managers whose decisions and behaviours will most shape the constituent parts of the employer brand mix.
- Tracking the right employee measures and facilitating management discussion on the performance gaps remaining between the current and desired employer brand experience.

Introducing a systematic approach to employer brand management should not cost the organisation more than good HR management. It need not necessarily replace anything you're doing well already, but simply help to bring the parts together to greater effect. On the contrary, as we argued in Chapter 7, effective employer brand management should result in significant savings in recruitment and retention, and promote a more engaged and productive workforce.

While many professional HR Directors should be capable of taking up the challenges we have described, a number of organisations are beginning to appoint 'employer brand managers' whose main remit is to co-ordinate between functions. Many of the current people who hold this title have moved into HR from marketing, or vice versa. Either way the individual must be a change agent, and command respect across the board for their integrity, energy and ability to listen. Brand management is about diplomacy and the art of the possible, and certainly not a role for the faint-hearted. Just as brand management transformed the way in which marketing was organised, we believe employer brand management can enhance HR's contribution to the business and the careers of those within it. We strongly believe that it is potentially the most attractive role in HR and indeed what HR should be about. But then we are biased!

SUMMARY

1. Building a strong employer brand requires more than consistent communication of the promise. It also requires careful and coherent management of the many different elements that shape employees' everyday experience of the brand.

2. There is no ideal template for an employer brand. An employer brand needs to be shaped to match the objectives and the resources of the organisation.

3. The employer brand 'mix' refers to the wide range of constituent elements that shape people's employment experience. These can be divided into two groups, relating to wider organisational context and policy, and local context and practice.

4. Every element within the employer brand 'mix' should reflect the underlying proposition and values and reinforce the desired brand experience.

5. Introducing a systematic approach to employer brand management disciplines should not cost more than good HR management.

6. Employer brand management is a task that most HR functions should be capable of performing in close conjunction with their counterparts in Marketing and Communication. However, a number of organisations have found it useful to create a specific employer brand management role to coordinate these cross-functional efforts.

7. As the following case studies demonstrate, employer brand management is not for the faint-hearted, but as we have also consistently found, fortune favours the brave!

The Durability of the Employer Brand Concept 12

Many new management disciplines have risen to prominence over the last 20 years. The pattern is now familiar. First there is the seminal book heralding a new dawn of management effectiveness. Consultancies appear on the market with well-packaged implementation programmes. There are a flurry of articles, conferences and guidebooks featuring competing models and pioneering case studies. In some cases there may even be an awards programme. Then, just as people are settling down to await the results, the fickle wheel of management fortune takes another turn, and there's a new game in town. Is employer branding, therefore, just another fad? We certainly don't believe so, and I would like to close this book with three fundamental reasons why we believe the discipline of employer brand management is here to stay.

1. *Organisations increasingly recognise that they cannot take the commitment and loyalty of their employees for granted* – Despite the desire to ensure that employees are broadly satisfied with their working conditions, it has largely been taken for granted that if you give people a decent job they will gratefully do your bidding. This view is increasingly at odds to the growing reality of employment. Leading companies are beginning to realise that valued employees, like profitable customers, are free to make choices, to join, to engage, to commit, and to stay. They are also beginning to realise that to attract the right kind of people, to encourage them to remain loyal and to perform to the best of their abilities requires a much more focused, coherent and benefit-led approach than has generally been provided in the past. Given the long-term trend for organisations to treat their valued employees more like valued customers, we believe that the logical conclusion for most will be to sharpen up the way

in which they manage the brand that these people work for – the employer brand.

2. *Employer branding provides an effective commercial bridge between HR, internal communications and marketing* – People management has long been the poor cousin of marketing management, with HR regarded by many organisations as an administrative cost centre rather than as a vital component in the creation and delivery of business value. This is fast changing. Most businesses have woken up to the vital importance of recruiting, retaining and developing the right people. The service sector, particularly, has woken up to the fundamental importance of engaging employee commitment in delivering customer satisfaction and loyalty. The growing commercial emphasis of these activities is bringing HR and internal communication practice increasingly in line with the approaches and disciplines more commonly applied to the creation and delivery of external value – namely, marketing and brand management.

3. *Employer branding draws on a discipline that has proven lasting value in the marketplace* – Branding and brand management have evolved over time, but the central tenets of the discipline – that is, close attention to the needs and aspirations of the target audience, focus on benefits, competitive differentiation and the marshalling of a coherent and consistent brand experience – are as central to brand management today as they have ever been. The foremost reason why employer branding is here to stay is that, in driving and sustaining people's commitment and loyalty, there has been no more effective approach than brand management. No doubt it will involve a further evolution in brand management practice. We believe that HR has as much to offer marketing as marketing has to HR. Both sides can learn, both sides will benefit, and if, as we believe, the greatest net benefit will ultimately be to the business, then employer branding will be here to stay.

Mihail Gorbachov's ambassador to London once commented that 'glasnost and perestroika are doors that will never be shut'. Simon and I would like to believe the same will be true of the Employer Brand.

Part III

Appendices

Appendix 1: Reuters Case Study

Following the announcement of its first ever year of loss in 2003, Reuters embarked on a three-year process of transformation called Fast Forward. The people-focused workstream within this programme, dubbed 'Living FAST', sought to redefine employees' perceptions of the organisation and drive a new way of working. While not referred to by Reuters as such, we believe that Living FAST bears all the hallmarks of an effective employer brand programme, with a focused employer brand proposition, core values, integrated delivery framework and consistent brand management.

History

Reuters is one of the few high technology communication companies that can trace its origins to the mid-nineteenth century. Julius Reuter launched the business in 1849 to transmit stock prices between the German town of Aachen and Brussels in Belgium, using the most versatile long-distance communication device of the day – the carrier pigeon. Despite being better known to the public as a news agency, 90% of Reuters' revenue is derived from its financial information and transactions services rather than its supply of news and pictures to the world's media. With 15 000 employees working in almost 100 countries, Reuters supplies information, analysis and trading tools to nearly half a million people in the financial markets worldwide.

The Business Context

Reuters experienced significant growth through the 1980s and 1990s on the back of stock market deregulation around the world. While stock markets boomed, there was an apparently insatiable appetite for Reuters' trading systems and information products. By the end of the 1990s, coupled with strong regional autonomy and undisciplined diversification into new product areas and technology platforms, this growth had translated into a sprawling and highly complex organisation. If all appeared reasonably well in a booming market, the picture looked significantly less attractive when the global economic slowdown began in early 2000. To provide some insight into the state of the organisation at that time, Reuters was offering over 1300 products on a multitude of different technical platforms, while its principal global competitor, Bloomberg, was selling just one product on a single technical platform. In a marketplace that was increasingly demanding global consistency and ease of use, Reuters found itself in a highly vulnerable position, and as the economy tightened, Reuters' share price duly plummeted.

Taking the Lead

In June 2001 Reuters appointed a new Chief Executive, Tom Glocer, with a clear remit to turn the situation around. Tom Glocer was an internal hire. Having previously held the position of CEO Latin America, and then CEO for the Americas, he knew Reuters well. He described the Reuters he joined in 1993 as 'a confederation of sovereign city-states rather than a unified company'. While he was clear from the start that Reuters needed to make some tough 'structural' decisions to survive, he was also sensitive to the danger of destroying the 'special fabric' that defined so much of value within the Reuters' culture. The course that Tom Glocer followed over the next three years reflects this combination of hard-headed, rational pragmatism and emotional intelligence that tends to distinguish effective leaders.

The Organisational Change Programme

While the primary focus of this case study is the Fast Forward Programme that began in February 2003, the process of change that was initiated following Tom Glocer's appointment represented an important stage in Reuters' transformation from a devolved and highly fragmented organisation to a highly focused and more consistently managed 'employer brand'. The Organisational Change Programme (OCP) that was initiated soon after Tom Glocer took over as CEO established four global customer segments, restructured the geographic business units into sales and service channels, and integrated the main business support functions, such as technical development, product management and marketing, into global centres of excellence. Soon after this re-engineering was achieved, the markets turned down and Reuters was forced to embark on its first ever major redundancy programme, with 3000 of Reuters' 19 000 employees eventually losing their jobs between June 2001 and early 2003.

Culture and Values

Despite these cost reductions, Tom Glocer's sensitivity to the 'special fabric' of Reuters' culture meant that a significant amount of management time and effort went into redefining the company's core values in the context of the new organisational realities. This process had started back in April 2001 with an international conference for 90 senior managers. Prior to the conference, all of the participants had been provided with the results of an employee research exercise comprising a quantitative survey and focus groups. While this provided important insights into the issues that mattered most to employees, the approach taken to defining the values was more of a creative than an analytical exercise. As John Reid-Dodick, the leader of the OCP's 'People' workstream commented: 'We're a story telling culture, and that's how we approached the values.' Groups of managers were asked to recount stories from the organisation that they felt characterised Reuters at its best and worst and to capture the essence of those stories in a word or phrase that they then wrote in 'behavioural bubbles'. The positive stories and 'bubbles' that resonated most strongly with the participants as a whole were then crafted into draft values. Following an additional period of research during which these values were further explored, tested and refined with groups of employees in each region, seven values were launched at the senior management conference held at the end of 2001.

Barbarians at the Gates

The launch of these values was closely interlinked with the OCP's harder edged structural changes. In the context of the financial marketplace in which 'all hell was breaking loose', it is worthy of note that one of the highlights of this conference was a presentation made by Steven Bungay, a management consultant and military historian affiliated with Ashridge. This began with the opening scene of 'Gladiator'. For the non-film buffs among you, this scene pits an embattled Roman Army against a Germanic barbarian horde, with the former wielding their superior discipline and fire power to devastating effect to claim victory. Steven Bungay then explained how some (not all) of the values and practices of the Roman Army were relevant to Reuters if it was to survive in an increasingly hostile business environment. This included such insights as the Roman Army's ability to soak up innovative new tactics, technologies and fighting talent from different parts of the world and redeploy the best of them wherever they operated. It cast a whole new light on the objectives and aspirations of OCP. It may have been a particularly bloody metaphor, but it was highly impactful, and effective in making the point.

Integrating the Internal and External Brand

The values presented at the end of 2001 served to provide the leadership team with a number of important 'anchor-points' that needed to be kept in mind as the OCP took hold, but there was no overt communication of these values to the rest of the organisation at this stage of the change process. The emphasis at this point, as John Reid-Dodick, Head of Organisational Development, put it was 'doing stuff that demonstrated these values', rather than 'pounding people over the head with them'. At the same time the 'internal values' work was being conducted, the external Reuters brand was also receiving attention. While the Reuters brand was well known it was generally agreed that the positioning of the brand in the marketplace lacked clarity and the company's marketing communications lacked impact.

Research conducted in 2002 among Reuters' key customers had helped to generate a list of external brand values for Reuters that were both desirable and credible. Fortunately, these were 'not dissimilar' to the internal cultural values, but nevertheless there was enough of a difference to create potential confusion among employees. With the aspiration to create one unified set of internal and external values, the brand and culture teams came together, and in January 2003 finally 'knit them together, word for word'.

'Fast Forward'

While some progress had been made during 2002 in restructuring and downsizing the organisation, the economic climate had continued to worsen, and on 17 February 2003, Reuters announced a loss of £493 million, the first full-year loss in its history. In response, Reuters' CEO, Tom Glocer, told the financial analysts that he was accelerating the business transformation with a three-year change programme called 'Fast Forward'.

'Fast Forward' contained five business change workstreams which aimed to continue and further sharpen many of the initiatives already under way in the OCP, such as product simplification and reduction of the cost base. But, as Tom Glocer made clear, the challenge involved 'much more than changing our architecture. It means changing the Reuters culture as well'. To give this substance, Tom Glocer established a sixth workstream, 'Living Fast', which would seek to define what Reuters would come to mean to its employees, in terms of core values and ways of working. Recognising the critical importance of behaviour change in delivering the other workstreams successfully, Tom Glocer also announced that he would take a direct role in leading 'Living Fast'.

Distilling the Values

Less than a month after the announcement of the 'Fast Forward' programme, Tom Glocer convened a two-day meeting of the company's top 100 managers with culture change as a central focus. Tom hand-picked 20 of these senior managers to be part of a workshop that he would lead to define the core values that would underpin 'Fast Forward'. After the first day, this team had refined the list of integrated brand and cultural values created a few months earlier to a shortlist of six. Tom then demanded even more focus and simplicity, with a reduction of the shortlist to three core values. These were agreed to be: 'Speed', 'Accountability' and 'Teamwork'. When these were presented to the plenary group the following day, the feedback called for a more explicit focus on customers, so the team agreed to add 'Service' and recommended a final list of four core values, as follows:

- Fast – Work with passion, urgency, discipline and focus.
- Accountable – Be clear on performance, responsibilities, rewards and consequences.
- Service-driven – Understand customer needs and exceed expectations through personal commitment.
- Team – Share, challenge and trust.

Given the neat alignment of the final values with the overall 'Fast Forward' programme it may come as some surprise that the Reuters team didn't start with the acronym FAST, and retrofit the values. According to John Reid-Dodick, who was closely involved in facilitating much of the culture workshop, this is not the way it happened. The 'eureka moment' only hit the team on the second day when they were integrating the focus on customers and decided to replace 'Speed' with 'Fast' and to add 'Service-driven'. With the team gathered around, Tom Glocer then worked with David Schlesinger, one of the company's most seasoned journalists who now heads up global editorial operations, to make the final version as simple and as memorable as possible.

The 'Living FAST' Framework

With the values defined, Tom Glocer then put together a team to define a 'Fast Forward' workstream called 'Living FAST' that would activate and embed the FAST values. This team was made up of functional experts, including the global heads of organisational development, people development, employee communications, and strategy, as well as high-potential business unit and regional representatives. One of the first outputs from this team was the 'Living FAST' framework (Figure A1.1) which defined the relationships between the different elements impacting on employees' experience of the values.

Building on this conceptual framework, a plan was then developed which defined the key phases that the team believed would be required to activate and then embed 'Living FAST'.

Mobilisation

With so many redundancies over the preceding period, morale was generally low, and the 'Living FAST' team knew there was an urgent need to

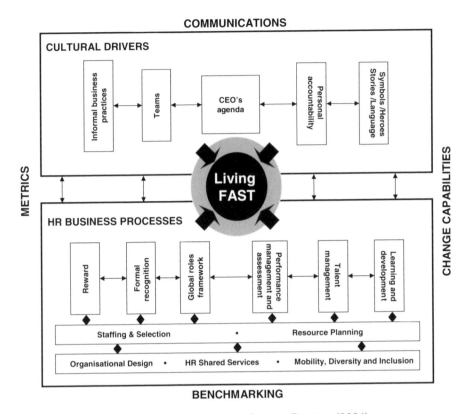

Figure A1.1 The 'Living FAST' framework. *Source:* Reuters (2004)

refocus employees on the active part they could play in securing a more positive future for Reuters. It turned out that the seed for this broader engagement had been planted at the senior management conference in March. Participants had left feeling highly energised and committed, and had been sharing their enthusiasm with employees in their business units as part of a planned communications cascade. In response, employees began asking how they could experience directly what had happened at the management conference.

To capitalise on this interest, the 'Living FAST' team considered various options, including a 'management conference' for a group of more junior employees or a global roadshow, but they decided that these would not reach enough people or would take too long. Then one of the members of the 'Living FAST' steering group, head of employee communications, Anne Marie Bell, floated a more radical approach. This entailed picking one day in June during which every Reuters employee would be given the opportunity to experience what was meant by 'Living FAST' and actively participate in making the transformation of Reuters a success. Initially dubbed 'Follow-the-Sun', the concept involved running a highly interactive and interconnected event, beginning on one side of the world with the rise of the sun, and following the sun from one time zone to the next for 24 hours, picking up every Reuters' site and employee along the way.

Anne Marie Bell recalls taking this idea to the steering group, and saying: 'I have this crazy idea. It's so crazy that it just might work.' The 'Living FAST' team loved the concept but were initially hesitant about taking on such an enormously difficult task. As the meeting progressed, and the team unpicked each of the knotty problems that they believed they might face, it began to dawn on them that it just might be possible to pull it off. The idea was taken to Chris Verougstraete, the Group HR Director, who was enthusiastic about an outreach to all employees and gave it his endorsement if they could secure the budget. The final call was then made by Tom Glocer. Anne Marie Bell recalls sending a note which read something along the lines of: 'I think this could be a real turning point. We need a million pounds to do it. If you think I'm crazy, you can fire me.' Tom Glocer's answer was short and to the point: 'Go do it.'

The Dream Team

In late April, with only six weeks' lead time, but the full support of the CEO, the 'Living FAST' team asked senior managers from around the world to nominate some of their highest potential people to the task. Tom Glocer sent out an invitation, and with five days' notice a diverse group of high performers was gathered in London to explore how the 'Follow-the-Sun' idea could be delivered. The task was spelled out on the first morning of the two-day workshop. Given that the response was generally one of incredulity and insecurity (what if it all goes wrong?), it was agreed that if by the end of the first day the assembled team still felt it was going to be impossible, then they would cancel the undertaking and think again. The participants worked on the task until midnight, breaking the challenge down into its component parts, and brainstorming potential solutions. By the close of the first day there was no question of turning back. By the end of the second day the team had a detailed implementation plan covering timings, logistics, roles, responsibilities and estimated costs.

Chris Verougstraete, the new Group HR Director who had joined Reuters a month previously as an expert in change management, came along to the workshop at the end of the second day and was 'simply blown away' by what the team had produced. Chris helped to sell the plan to the leadership team the following Monday, and 'June 11', as the event simply came to be known, was on.

Preparing for 'June 11'

As soon as the 'Dream Team' members returned to their business units they were tasked with creating a network of volunteers who would help to plan and run the 'June 11' event locally. These local efforts were coordinated and supported by a section of the new 'Living FAST' website called 'In the Know'. There were also numerous conference calls arranged, one of which was led by Tom Glocer himself. With the active involvement of the CEO and the 'buzz' around the event growing day by day, hundreds of employees volunteered to take an active role.

To further engage employees prior to the event, Reuters also launched an 'Issues Audit' on the 'Living FAST' website, designed to enable employees to log any issues that they felt required management attention. This proved to be a highly popular initiative with over 1900 issues logged on the site in the weeks leading up to the event.

'This is One for the Books on How to Communicate'

The 'June 11' event, beginning in Australia and ending in California 24 hours later, comprised six core components:

1. A multimedia opening event hosted by senior managers to introduce employees to 'Fast Forward' and the FAST values.
2. A cross-functional 'Living FAST' session in which all 15000 employees got together in groups of 10–15 people to identify specific

ways that the company as a whole, and they as individuals, could help to embed the FAST values.

3. A functional team-based session focused on tackling the 23 most substantial issues generated by the issues audit. This session, called 'Tom's Challenges' involved managers choosing the challenges they would address with their teams, ranging from reducing e-mail overload, running more effective meetings through to bigger organisational issues, such as promoting the Reuters brand more effectively.

4. An internal news channel created by Reuters' in-house television experts, featuring 20 hours of programming, 94 scheduled live appearances, including Q&A sessions with Tom Glocer, and 80 pre-recorded items.

5. A variety of fun and social activities, many of which raised money for charities supported by the company's charitable fund, the Reuters Foundation.

6. 150 stories filed to the 'Living FAST' website, edited by a Reuters' journalist working in the employee communications function.

Even with a tightly scheduled framework, detailed facilitation guidelines, a backbone of pre-recorded film clips and regional piloting of some of the core components, the event largely relied on the local senior managers and 'Living FAST' volunteers to bring it all together on the day. It worked. There were no major technical glitches. The TV anchorman, Steve Clarke, a seasoned network TV professional, led 14 hours of the 20 hours' programming. The interactive sessions generated both heated discussion and productive output. And, very importantly, the event was clearly enjoyed by the majority of those participating. It lifted people's heads from the painful redundancies, and refocused them on building a company that will protect the remaining jobs. It re-ignited people's pride in the company ('one of the few companies in the world that could pull this kind of event off'). It rebuilt confidence in a management team that was clearly prepared to both invest in its people, and take the time to listen to them.

The following e-mail from a senior executive who had recently joined Reuters from one of its competitors, where he had been CEO, gives some impression of the response:

> I just wanted to say that you achieved something really incredible yesterday. To attempt to pull off the technical feat alone was brave, but to deliver

a substantial program that pulled together an entire 15,000 strong global company was just awesome.

Message, delivery, collaboration, energy and motivation were all on target. This is one for the books on how to communicate. Thank you for a great day, you should be proud. I believe there are thousands around the world who, thanks to your efforts, were proud to see the company and its capability on display.

Responding to Employee Input

The issues audit and subsequent 'June 11' workshops had invited the points of view of every Reuters' employee, but as anyone who had participated in this kind of listening exercise will tell you, judgement is generally suspended until these points of view receive a considered management response. Tom Glocer was clear on this requirement, and demanded that every issue receive a response within 3 weeks. The final issue bank containing 3400 items of employee feedback was posted on the 'Living FAST' website, and each issue was given a number and assigned a manager as the 'accountable owner' responsible for posting a written response by the deadline. The response had to resolve the issue immediately, set out a clear rationale for why it would not be addressed, or provide an appropriate plan of action for how it would be resolved over time. This was a tough process to complete. As one of the response coordinators commented: 'it felt like we were a snake trying to digest a porcupine'. Nevertheless the three week promise was delivered. Moreover, as a tangible demonstration of the 'accountable' aspect of the FAST values, managers who had proposed plans of action had to report on progress over the following months, and that progress was rated on the 'Living FAST' website as either 'green', 'amber', or 'red' until it was completed.

While at times the audit exercise felt to those involved like 'boiling the ocean for a cupful of salt' it was recognised as having played an invaluable role in enthusing people for the 'June 11' event. The fact that the audit was completely open and uncensored helped to reinforce the honesty and integrity of the programme, and generated an enormous amount of interest in the goals and ongoing progress of 'Living FAST'. Such was the popularity of the issues audit that, when it was finally closed down, many people requested a more permanent channel for raising and discussing issues. The result was the reconfiguration of an existing intranet channel,

'TalkBack', providing a new 'one stop shop' for raising issues and sharing ideas.

The Main Effort Plan

In mid-July 2003, Tom Glocer again had the 'Living FAST' team convene a group of high potential employees, this time to use the 'June 11' feedback to develop a clear and well-founded plan of action for driving culture change in the company. In advance of the two-day meeting, each participant was provided with a synopsis of the principal themes that emerged from the issues audit and was encouraged to review the issues and responses on the 'Living FAST' website. Recognising that culture change on the scale required could only happen over time, the group were asked to identify a small number of company-wide priorities and to develop a 'main effort plan' to phase and sequence those efforts under the banner of 'Living FAST'.

The group worked late into the night on the first day to prepare their recommendations for Tom Glocer, who joined them for three hours the following morning. He engaged in a spirited exchange – asking detailed questions, exploring alternative points of view, and encouraging the group to keep things as simple as possible. Noting the company's tendency for complexity and fondness for acronyms, Tom at one point joked that the group's challenge was to come up with a plan that would avoid employee 'MYGO' ('My eyes glaze over'). The result was the Main Effort Plan (Figure A1.2).

This plan identified four distinct phases, each with a small number of core deliverables. The 'Things are Changing' phase had begun with 'June 11' and evolved further by engaging employees through improved management change capability and broader communications efforts. The second and perhaps most challenging phase was 'Getting Simpler', which sought to clarify business unit objectives and link them more directly with individual objectives; to create a simpler and more aligned organisation; and to help employees to gain a much better understanding of who does what in the organisation. The 'Knowing Our Customers' phase was to enable employees to better understand Reuters' business, which straddles the media, technology, and financial services sectors, and to improve customer service by enhancing the quality of service that

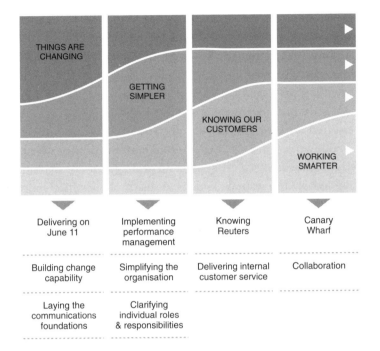

Figure A1.2 The Main Effort Plan. *Source:* Reuters (2004)

employees themselves experience from the company. The 'Working Smarter' phase sought to integrate the FAST values into plans to consolidate most London-based employees into a single location in Canary Wharf during 2005, and to focus on achieving greater collaboration among employees globally.

MANAGING THE 'LIVING FAST' BRAND

While 'Living FAST' originated as a workstream within the wider 'Fast Forward' programme, it soon became clear that it had the potential to become a powerful focus for employees' relationship with the 'new' Reuters that they were now engaged in building. It was decided at an early stage to develop a distinct look and feel for 'Living FAST' and produce guidelines that would help to ensure that the 'Living FAST' brand was carefully managed to retain its clarity of focus and maximise its impact. In this context, strict rules were applied to how the brand could be applied. Managers were dissuaded wherever possible from using the new 'Living FAST' identity to liven up their business-as-usual communications (particularly following the success of 'June 11'). This helped to ensure a clear distinction between the old ways and the new and maintain the integrity and meaning of 'Living FAST'.

This required a major overhaul of the internal communications infrastructure. Following 'June 11' the internal communications function was centralised and rationalised to ensure greater global consistency. While still 'embedded' in the regions and local units, the internal communications function began to be managed as a global team. While this initially met with resistance from the local line management, they soon realised several clear benefits in addition to the more consistent management of 'Living FAST'. There was less 'noise' in the internal communications channels. The issues audit had surfaced a general dissatisfaction with the volume, inconsistency and multiple layering of the previous communications infrastructure. Tighter management from the centre meant fewer, more consistent and more clearly constructed messages. Working as a global team also meant that Reuters could leverage its coverage across time zones more effectively. The Daily Briefing, an online internal news update, was previously criticised for being too static and too UK centric. The Daily Briefing could now be updated several times a day carrying news from one region to the next around the clock. The global connectivity of the team also meant that the local line managers felt closer to the CEO's agenda and more able to influence the global agenda via their local communications representative.

The issues audit also helped to drive home improvements in the internal communications channels. The combination of powerful technology platforms and highly creative IT managers had resulted in much of the intranet being 'sexy but difficult to navigate and to use'. The audit demanded greater clarity and simplicity and this helped to drive a reduction in web sites from 1300 to 200, and a more 'fit for purpose' approach to developing and managing content.

These improvements to the communications infrastructure both supported the tight management of 'Living FAST' messages, and substantiated them in terms of delivering greater focus, more effective service and enhanced global team working.

KNOW. NOW

Reuters' external brand was one of the key points of discussion during the 'June 11' workshops. It was generally felt that Reuters was a great brand, but the company was under-investing in this vital asset compared to key competitors like Bloomberg. On 'June 11', the global marketing team literally 'worked around the clock' on the most effective way forward, and building on much of the work conducted the previous year, committed to a brand relaunch in the early Autumn of 2003. The new brand positioning that resulted from this work focused on Reuters' unique ability to bring together all the information sources, tools and access that their customers needed to act fast and with confidence. The new external brand proposition, summed up in the new tag line 'Know. Now', was felt to address the needs of the customer in a concise and impactful way, and to further reinforce the organisational values of 'Living FAST'.

With the success of 'June 11' still fresh in mind, the marketing team used a number of similar techniques to launch 'Know. Now' internally a week before the new campaign was launched externally. Local senior management teams were equipped with everything they needed to brief their teams (including presentations, scripts, and copies of the forthcoming advertising campaign) and run workshop style sessions to invite people's ideas and support behind delivering the external brand promise. The positive reception that the marketing campaign received internally, despite continued cost cutting and redundancies in other areas, was a further testament to the power of employee communication and involvement in winning support for change.

Embedding the Values

While the style and intent of the 'June 11' event, the issues audit and response, and the subsequent 'Know. Now' briefings had done much to embody the FAST values, the step that probably had the greatest effect on making the FAST values real for people was to incorporate them into the performance management system. In the issues audit and 'June 11' workshop sessions, employees had called for feedback on their performance that (a) reflected broader input than just that of their immediate manager and (b) focused on 'how' they worked and not just on 'what' they achieved. Anne Bowerman, a member of the 'Living FAST' core team and head of the learning and development function in HR, responded by incorporating 'FAST Feedback' into the performance management process. The new approach, launched in October 2003, involved a 360-degree component in which employees nominate 6–8 colleagues to provide their reviewing managers with input on specific ways in which the employees exhibit the FAST values. The managers consolidate the 'FAST Feedback', include a FAST rating in performance review forms, and discuss the themes with employees during review meetings. The approach to performance management also changed. While formal reviews are still held once a year, there is now much more emphasis on informal performance feedback quarterly, or even monthly.

'Fast Forward' targets have been incorporated into executive bonus awards, and into a global 'Living FAST' recognition scheme, which publicly rewards exemplary performance according to the FAST values

Knowing Reuters, Knowing Our Customers

During 'June 11' Tom Glocer had committed to another event the following year. Given the pace of change that the organisation had experienced over the intervening period, it was decided that the June event in 2004 should act as a re-induction programme for Reuters' employees. With the primary focus on how Reuters delivers value to its customers, Reuters created an Expo style programme of events with exhibitions in seven locations around the world and via the intranet. Following a briefing on the progress that had been made since 'June 11', employees were then given the opportunity to contribute to 18 separate stands where they could receive a further briefing on different elements of the Reuters' business and it primary customer segments. Recognising that people were likely to start with different levels of understanding, the event offered a flexible approach, with employees left to decide which stands they felt would offer them greatest value. This programme was supported with both business TV and web-based e-learning programmes for those unable to attend the Expo and for people who wanted to extend or reinforce what they had picked up from the Expo experience.

Measuring Success

In the survey carried out in November 2004, 87% of employees said they fully support the values for which Reuters stands. In the first year of 'Fast Forward', there was a nine-point increase in the percentage of employees who felt Reuters had a well-formulated strategy for the present, and that measure increased a further six points in the November 2004 survey. This employee confidence in the 'Fast Forward' programme was also borne out by the company's results. The reported figures for 2003 saw the Group return to profit, and Reuters' shares increased in value by 60% during 2004, making it was one of the strongest performers in the FTSE 100 that year.

Culture change on this scale is not for the faint-hearted. Events dictated that it acts decisively and its coherent, integrated approach gave it the best chance possible to meet its targets for recovery in the short term, and create an enterprise more responsive to market challenges and opportunities into the future.

Appendix 2: Tesco Case Study

With over 960 stores and 230 000 employees, Tesco has risen to become the most dominant supermarket chain in the UK and the most successful at exporting this success into international markets. Tesco's leadership team claim that the company's growing market share and profitability are directly connected to the superior service customers receive from its employees. The high levels of employee satisfaction and commitment that underpin this performance have, in turn, been supported by the development of a powerful employer brand proposition and values that provide consistent touchstones for every management action that impacts on the employee experience.

The Business Context

In 1992 it was a different story. Tesco was Britain's second biggest supermarket chain, but struggling. European discount stores were beginning to make inroads into Britain, and investment analysts feared that the young profile of Tesco's customer base would put them at greater danger than their main rivals. Tesco's share price fell by 40%.

It was the year that the future CEO, Terry Leahy, was appointed marketing director. As he recalls: 'It was a defining period and from that time we began to change the philosophy and direction of the business.' Tesco's recovery strategy was to listen more carefully to customers and drive innovation to meet their needs better than any other retailer.

Transforming the Customer Experience

In the next few years, under the new marketing tagline 'Every Little Helps', Tesco introduced over 100 new initiatives to improve the shopping experience of its customers. These included the first ever nationwide customer loyalty scheme, 'Clubcard', the 'One in Front' checkout system designed to minimise queuing time, and a series of price-cutting initiatives, including a new 'Value Line' range. Tesco's strategy to invest in hypermarkets, at a time when its main rival, Sainsbury's, stuck to its mid-sized supermarket formula, also proved to be a vital component in its subsequent rise to pre-eminence.

Customer Insight Unit

The year 1995, in which Tesco overtook Sainsbury's to become the UK's leading grocery retailer, was also marked by the creation of its Customer Insight Unit (CIU). Moving beyond the conventional market research unit, the CIU represented the first retail department of its type in the UK to draw together all the previous fragmentary sources of customer information, including the increasingly sophisticated analysis of 'Clubcard' data, that could throw light on the attitudes, behaviours, needs and aspirations of its customers.

Terry Leahy and the First Values Programme

When Terry Leahy was appointed the new CEO in 1997, he took over a company that was on the up. He also realised that there was still a long way to go. Leahy was adamant that Tesco needed to establish a way of working that would keep it ahead of its competitors and that, to support this, Tesco needed to clarify its values. Following a significant period of employee research and management consultation, Tesco introduced five core values and eight people statements in a relatively low key way during the summer of 1997.

- *Core Value Statements*
    1. Understand customers better than anyone.
    2. Be energetic, innovative and take risks in making life better for customers.
    3. Use intelligence, scale and technology to deliver unbeatable values to customers in everything we do.
    4. Recognise that we have brilliant people, use this strength to make our customers' shopping enjoyable in a way no competitor can.

5. Earn the respect of our staff for the values and appreciate their contribution;

- *People Statements*
  1. Tesco people are all retailers, there's one team, the Tesco team.
  2. Tesco people reward their staff for creating value for customers.
  3. Tesco people are encouraged to take risks, give support and don't blame.
  4. Tesco people talk to their staff, listen to what they say and share knowledge so that it can be used.
  5. Tesco people trust and respect each other.
  6. Tesco people respect all customers, the community, suppliers and competition.
  7. Tesco people strive for personal excellence in everything we do – we leave no stone unturned in order to do it right.
  8. Tesco people have fun, celebrate success and learn from failure.

This internal launch was supported with posters and credit card sized cards, but as a senior Tesco manager later admitted, there was no real infrastructure to support the values and 'no pain for not living them'.

Soon after the launch, Tesco's employee survey, 'Viewpoint', was used to benchmark the degree to which employees currently associated the company with these core values and people statements. The findings indicated that Tesco had significant challenges to address if it was to meet the aspirations defined in many of these statements. The most positive employee associations with Tesco were those relating to customers. For example, 84% associated 'respecting our customers', 82% 'delivering the best value to customers' and 75% 'taking chances to exceed customer needs', with working for Tesco. However, only 40% of employees believed that what they did was valued by the company, only 43% felt 'valued by their immediate Manager/Supervisor' and only 44% associated 'being listened to and having your opinion valued' with working for Tesco. A summary report at the time concluded that few of the employee-centred values were particularly positive.

Re-addressing the Values

While some progress was made in addressing the key issues underlying these findings during the course of 1998, the most significant breakthroughs followed the appointment of a dedicated Values Manager, Jo Baily, in early 1999. Results from the latest 'Viewpoint' survey continued to reveal that employees felt less valued than customers. Having already recognised a strong link between customer satisfaction and employees' perceptions that 'we look after our people', the management team at Tesco knew this imbalance needed more attention. In response to frequent criticisms that the values were too complicated, both in terms of their number and 'management speak' language, Tesco set out again to consult with employees to help to identify a set of values that would resonate more strongly with the organisation as a whole. During this period, active senior support was evident with the Board meeting three times just to discuss the 'values'. The result was two core values, and a shortened and more concisely worded list of supporting value statements, as follows:

1. *'No-one tries harder for customers'*
   - Understand customers better than anyone
   - Be energetic, be innovative and be first for customers
   - Use our strengths to deliver unbeatable value for customers
   - Look after our people so they can look after our customers
2. *'Treat people as we like to be treated'*
   - All retailers, there's one team . . . The Tesco Team
   - Give support to each other and praise more than criticise.
   - Ask more than tell, and share knowledge so that it can be used.
   - Trust and respect each other.
   - Strive to do our very best.
   - Enjoy work, celebrate success and learn from experience.

Embedding the Values

These values were the topic of Terry's keynote speech to the top 1500 Tesco managers in September 1999. This initial launch was then followed by a series of values workshops run for the next tier of managers by senior line management 'champions', and a wider communications cascade for general shop assistants. The values workshop programme attended by general shop assistants was positioned as one of eight modules in a wider training programme.

Drawing on their experience from the previous values programme, Tesco realised that embedding the values would require far more than a one-off briefing. One of the steps Tesco took to help managers to internalise these values was to incorporate them into a new 360-degree feedback process which covered: living the values, delivering for customers and 'taking people with them'. An award scheme for living the values was also established for staff, with people encouraged to make awards to anyone they felt demonstrated the values, with a copy posted to the recipients' line manager. While there was some initial cynicism, this became a very popular initiative among staff and managers alike.

The Employer Brand Proposition

In January 2001, David Fairhurst joined Tesco as Resourcing Director with a remit to look at every aspect of the Tesco offer to employees. Drawing on his experience from Smithkline Beecham, where he had developed and implemented a successful employer brand strategy, David set out to build on the values programme with a broader, more holistic approach to managing the employee experience of Tesco.

With help from members of the CIU, Tesco established a People Insight Unit (PIU), and set about achieving a similar level of insight into their employees as they had with customers. Starting with a nationwide programme of focus groups with both employees and people from outside the company, Tesco ran a survey called 'Your Life . . . Your Future' which focused on what their employees most valued about working at Tesco, and their work–life aspirations for the future. The findings from this research helped Tesco to identify four leading factors that drove commitment to Tesco:

1. *Trust and respect* – The most important commitment driver for most employees was having a positive relationship with their workmates and manager.

2. *An interesting job* – The second most important commitment driver for many was the degree of interest they found in the jobs they performed.

3. *The opportunity to get on* – This related to the opportunity to improve on their current pay package and benefits, and advance their career.

4. *A boss who supports me* – This related to the general level of support people received in terms of communication with their line manager, control over their workload, and opportunities for training and development.

This became the 'employee shopping list' of priorities, matching the 'shopping list' of key priorities Tesco had earlier defined for customers. Together with the core values, these four employee priorities became the guiding principles for developing a more coherent employer brand proposition for employees.

The Steering Wheel

Both the 'Customer' proposition and the 'People' [employer brand] proposition are incorporated within a management tool that Tesco call the 'Steering Wheel' (Figure A2.1). The Steering Wheel lies at the heart of the company's business planning strategy, with 'Financial' and 'Operations' making up two further quadrants. Tesco uses this 'balanced scorecard' framework to define its goals and deliverables. They have stated that in 'being customer focused, efficient in our operations and keeping our people at the heart of all we do' the finance delivers itself. Each segment sets the business priorities for the year ahead and is driven and monitored by Key Performance Indicators (KPIs), which set 'challenging but achievable' targets for the business. Each KPI is backed by a business case, quantifying the expected benefits, and owned by a specific director.

The Steering Wheel is linked to the objectives of all employees, linking strategy to their everyday work. The Steering Wheel is also displayed in every department and store, with a simple traffic light system used to indicate whether they are on track. The KPIs are measured and reported to the Board each quarter, with a summary report sent to the top 2000 managers to cascade to their staff.

Delivering on the Employer Brand Promises

The 'People' segments of the Steering Wheel represent the core focus of the 'People Plan', which shapes many of the critical factors influencing the employee relationship with Tesco, such as remuneration and

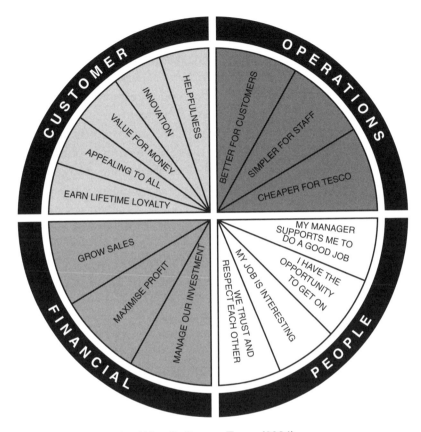

Figure A2.1 The 'Steering Wheel'. *Source:* Tesco (2004)

reward, management development, training, performance management, internal communication and recruitment. This plan is owned by the group HR function, and informed by fortnightly meetings of a cross-Functional 'People Matters Group', who help to monitor the progress of the 'People Plan'.

My Manager Supports Me to Do a Good Job

HR policies and processes are highly centralised at Tesco, with each store governed by a detailed routines handbook closely specifying how each task should be performed. While this plays an important role in creating the framework for employer brand management, it is widely recognised that the most critical factor in delivering the employer brand experience is how middle managers and supervisors interact with their staff on an everyday basis. This belief was reinforced by a research study conducted in 2003. A team of independent researchers were asked to study four Tesco supermarkets located in similar towns, one a high performer, one a low performer and two average performers. The team were unaware of the financial performance of each store when they conducted the research, but were spot on when asked to identify the relative ranking of each store in terms of performance after they had conducted their study. The high-performing store recorded significantly higher employee satisfaction with HR policies, their line managers and the level of influence they had over their own jobs. The scores on all four of these dimensions were significantly lower in the poorly performing store. Interestingly, the average performers recorded similarly high levels of commitment to Tesco as an employer, but scored less well on satisfaction with line managers and job influence. The conclusions from this 'Black Box' study were clear. From Tesco's perspective it supported their belief that the strongest factor impacting customer satisfaction was employees, and the strongest factor impacting employees was the store manager.

Tesco's approach to driving higher quality people management at store level has incorporated four main thrusts.

1. Highly targeted management recruitment (based on attitude as well as skills).
2. Ensuring that managers understand and share the core values.
3. High levels of investment in training and development, with a strong emphasis on management style (particularly high visibility and approachability).
4. Continual assessment of management competence through performance review, 360-degree feedback and employee survey measures.

Following the values roll-out in 1999, Tesco embarked on a significant programme of retraining for all 12 000 managers. This training equipped them to define people's roles more clearly, provide greater support to front-line staff, communicate better, and address the factors that would make work more satisfying and the workplace more effective.

There has also been a consistent emphasis in recent years to 'turn the organisation upside down', as one senior executive put it, so that the leadership team see their role as supporting the wider management team rather than imposing solutions on them, and expect managers to treat their own staff accordingly. To reinforce the value placed on understanding and supporting front-line personnel, head office managers are encouraged to make regular store visits. Leahy led from the front in making this a priority by signing up to spend a week working in-store on the checkout, at the fish counter and in the warehouse.

Tesco also discovered that one of the biggest factors obstructing the store managers from getting on and managing their staff effectively was perceived to be the significant amounts of time they felt they had to spend 'making sense' of the multitude of initiatives sent in their direction from head office. The current HQ mantra, reflected in the 'Operations' quadrant of the Steering Wheel, is 'Better for customers', 'Simpler for staff', and 'Cheaper for Tesco'. More rigorous application of this filter to new initiatives has helped significantly in cutting down the load and freeing up store managers' time to 'look after people so they can look after our customers'.

The Opportunity to Get on

Tesco puts a great deal of emphasis in sharing its financial success with its employees. As Terry Leahy has said, 'There has been a very significant increase in the pay of all our people, paid for by big increases in productivity. We pay them as well as we can and they are very motivated.' Average pay for staff in stores is now higher than all its competitors and there are a range of other wealth-sharing schemes. Tesco's 'Save as you earn' scheme, open to all staff completing one year's service, has delivered significant returns to those participating since it was first established in 1999. The schemes offered to Tesco staff in October 2002 attracted over 63 000 applications. Tesco also runs a profit share scheme that recently distributed £38 million worth of shares to 75 000 employees.

In addition to 'getting on' financially, Tesco also has a strong belief in promoting from within. David Fairhurst, Tesco's global resourcing director, continues to stress that wherever possible the company promotes from within to fill new posts. This is supported by a staff-training package ('Bronze, Silver, Gold') and talent-spotting programme that helps to identify and develop management potential.

Trust and Respect

Trust and respect lie at the heart of Tesco's core people value: 'Treat people as we like to be treated.' Developing the behaviours that support this value are a key component in Tesco management training and evaluation. Trust and respect are also demonstrated by means of the wide range of forums provided for employees to express their opinions and ideas. In addition to the 'Viewpoint' survey, Tesco runs regular briefing and discussion sessions for in-store staff and participation in Tesco's ideas and suggestions schemes are high, reflecting the regular implementation of staff-generated improvement ideas.

Employee Segmentation and Flexible Offerings

Customer segmentation is a powerful marketing tool that Tesco have used to great effect. Analysing data from its 10 million Tesco Clubcard holders, Tesco has tailored its offering to major subgroups within the market through its 'Finest', 'Fair Trade', 'Organic', 'Healthy Living' and 'Value' ranges. It is typical of Tesco's 'joined-up' management approach that it has begun to apply similar tools and techniques to tailoring its employment offer to different subgroups of employees.

Combining data from the Viewpoint census survey with the findings from 'Your life . . . Your Future' survey, the People Insight Unit identified five attitudinal segments, representing different attitudes towards employment. The two most common types were found to be: *'Work–Life Balancers'*, who placed more importance on flexible working than promotion, and *'Want It All'* employees, the most ambitious and demanding group, whose loyalty was dependent on good money, good prospects for promotion and challenging work. The group forecast to most increase in size over the coming years was the *'Pleasure Seekers'*, who generally appeared to take more interest in their leisure time than pride in their work.

Tesco believes that this kind of analysis foreshadows a new strategic direction for motivation strategy, and has increasingly sought to tailor benefits, recognition and other incentive policies around specific employee types, groups and preferences. This includes offering cash alternatives to peripheral benefits such as company cars, life assurance and private health schemes. Tesco details each package in personalised benefits statements, so all employees understand the value of the benefits that are provided. It has helped to identify new forms of incentive, such as the 'holiday discount club', which was expected to be highly motivating to a significant number of staff. It has also prompted a greater focus on flexibility. Tesco's reward manager Richard Sullivan commented that 'There has been a swing away from the importance of the financial package. I am seeing more people taking career breaks, going part time and so on, and it is important that the company supports these kinds of activities.'

Diversity

A further aspect of Tesco's desire to understand the different needs and aspirations of its employees has been reflected in the research conducted to underpin its diversity policy. For example, Tesco has recently completed an important study evaluating the primary motivations of its older (50+) employees, having recognised the growing importance of this age group in the labour market, and the distinct benefits they can potentially bring to the workplace.

Measurement of Success

Tesco's most recent 'Viewpoint' staff survey recorded staff satisfaction at an all time high of 81%. This 'Viewpoint' survey was also the first to show a positive green light (on the traffic light scale) for all Tesco's values, in all its divisions, since the values were first established in 1997. Tesco enjoys some of the best employee retention rates in the retail sector, with their latest published figures claiming an annual turnover of 18% for store employees, 7% for distribution and 8% for head office (for all staff with more than one year's service).

The figures from Tesco's regular customer panels, which include questions on employee behaviour and service, demonstrate high levels of praise for staff attitudes, underpinning consistently high levels of customer satisfaction.

Tesco's winning combination of great customer brand, great people brand, and tight operational and financial management have helped it to generate significant year on year business growth since 1997, with a record 16.3% increase in sales and full year profit of £1.6 billion for the year ending February 2004. Terry Leahy, CEO, stated:

It takes a generation. We've had to change completely the way we manage. Change at Tesco has been across the board, but internally coherent . . . What's important is that you live the values. They have to be central to the way you manage in order to affect processes and projects, and how people work . . . It's been evolution, not revolution. Rapid evolution.

Appendix 3: Extract from Greggs' Performance Development Review Guidance Notes (2004)

USING VALUES WITHIN THE REVIEW DISCUSSION

Manager's Checklist

1. **Enthusiastic** (keen, positive and willing)
   - The review is important to individuals – it's quality time spent with their manager focusing solely on them as individuals. They will also have spent time preparing for the meeting.
   - This might be the eighth review you've conducted in the last two weeks but you still need to be as enthusiastic about the last as the first!
   - Be keen to take on board the views of the individual.
   - Prepare properly for each review, not just the documentation but consider the environment. Have you allocated sufficient time, is the venue suitable for the individual, have you ensured that there will be no phone interruptions?

2. **Supportive** (good listener, helpful, encouraging)
   - Listen to what the individual has to say – both facts and feelings.
   - Encourage the individual to reflect on performance and learning points.
   - Listen to what the individual says and doesn't say. Remember to use the skills of questioning and active listening – concentrate on this review, not the next one you're doing!

3. **Open and honest** (truthful, trustworthy, approachable, open minded)
   - Be open and honest with the individual in terms of his/her performance and aspirations.
   - Encourage the individual to 'open-up' to you.
   - Keep an open mind yourself – don't prejudge situations without fully listening to all the facts – sometimes we can be wrong!
   - Individuals may pick up on some things that you haven't considered – be receptive! It might well be a better idea or a valid point.

4. **Consideration** (thinking of others, being understanding, caring for people and the environment)
   - Consider the manner in which you have to deliver certain messages and balance with being open and honest.
   - When booking the time, consider whether it's suitable for both you and the individual. Ensure that it doesn't clash with other commitments.
   - Think of the time you have allocated, particularly if it is the first time you have used the new process. Ensure that it is sufficient (approximately 3 hours).
   - Don't overbook the number of reviews you do in a day. Not only will it affect the quality of time you spend with each individual, but think of yourself – you will be exhausted by the end!

5. **Respect** (valuing individuals, treating others as they would wish to be treated)
   - Again consider your approach when delivering difficult messages.
   - Value individuals for the contribution they are making to overall business success – and tell them!

6. **Fairness** (no favouritism, consistent, seeing from both sides)
   - Be aware of your own prejudices. Don't focus on one aspect or the latest situation. Remember the review is about overall performance over the last 12 months.
   - Always consider the facts of the situation – apply the role profile measures and ratings consistently across your team.
   - Consider the whole team when setting objectives – look at development need, not working relationship!
   - Ensure that opportunities are open to all and applied equally.

7. **Appreciative** (saying thank you and recognising achievement)
   - Individuals will have put a lot of time into preparing for their review. Thank them for their time and contribution!
   - Recognise each individual's achievement and say so!
   - If individuals have performed well – praise them, recognising their contribution to the business.

Checklist for Individuals Participating in a Review

1. **Enthusiastic** (keen, positive and willing)
   - Be prepared to get fully involved – remember it's a two-way process. Do your preparation and participate fully in the review itself.
   - Value the one-to-one time you will be spending with your manager. Have a positive approach – your manager is spending this time for your benefit!
   - Think of the outcomes in a positive way. Have a 'can do' mentality not 'I won't be able to achieve this'.
2. **Supportive** (good listener, helpful, encouraging)
   - Listen to the feedback you are receiving, both the facts and the way your manager might be feeling.
   - Recognise that while you might be seeking support from your manager, equally you may be asked to support others. Be prepared to help!
3. **Open and honest** (truthful, trustworthy, approachable, open minded)
   - Use this opportunity to be open with your manager about how you feel – both the good things and the not so good things about the job. Equally, your manager will be telling you how she/he views your performance. Recognise that their view might be different to yours – be open minded with the feedback you receive.
   - 360-degree feedback is about other people's perceptions of you – again this may differ in some circumstances to your view. Be receptive to the comments made!
4. **Consideration** (thinking of others, being understanding, caring for people and the environment).
   - Consider your manager! Remember that while this is your only review, your manager could be responsible for conducting upwards of 8 to 10.

5. **Respect** (valuing individuals, treating others as they would wish to be treated)
   - If you have an issue to discuss with your manager, think about the way you put your point across.
6. **Fairness** (no favouritism, consistent, seeing from both sides)
   - Value your manager's opinion and those taking time to provide you with 360-degree feedback.
   - Try to learn from the information you are receiving.
7. **Appreciative** (saying thank you and recognising achievement)
   - Recognise the time your manager has taken in preparing for your review and those who have completed the 360-degree feedback. Thank them for their contribution.

References

Preface

1. Reeves, R. (1961) *Reality in Advertising*, Alfred Knopf, New York.
2. Ogilvy, D. (1963) *Confessions of an Advertising Man*, Atheneum, New York.
3. *The Economist* (2003) Employer Branding Survey.
4. Dell and Ainspan (2001) *Engaging Employees Through Your Brand*, The Conference Board, Research Report 1288-01-RR.
5. Ambler, T. and Barrow, S. (1996) 'The Employer Brand', *Journal of Brand Management*, 4 (3).

Chapter 1

1. Roddick, A. (1991) *Body and Soul*, Ebury Press, Random House Group.
2. Rushdie, S. (1980) *Midnight's Children*, Penguin, Harmondsworth, UK.
3. Ambler, T. and Barrow, S. (1996) 'The Employer Brand', *Journal of Brand Management*, 4 (3).

Chapter 2

1. Michaels, E., Handfield-Jones, H. and Axelrod, B. (2001) *The War for Talent*, Harvard Business School Press.
2. Rogers, S. (1859) *Recollections* (p. 215), William Sharpe, London.
3. Hamilton, N. (2001) *The Full Monty*, Allen Lane.
4. CBI Submission to the Low Pay Commission (1997).
5. Orwell, G. (1937) *The Road to Wigan Pier*, Victor Gollancz.
6. Sigal, C. (1960) *Weekend in Dinlock*, Secker & Warburg.
7. Lawrence, D.H. (1960) *Lady Chatterley's Lover*, Penguin.
8. Woodruff, W. (2000) *Road to Nab End*, Eland Publishing.
9. Eliot, T.S. (1922) *The Waste Land*, Boni & Liveright, New York.
10. Miller, A. (1949) *Death of a Salesman*, Penguin.
11. Fletcher, W. (1988) *Creative People: How to Manage Them and Maximize Their Creativity*, Hutchinson Business Books.
12. *Harvard Business Review* (July 2000) 'How to Manage Millionaires'.
13. *Attitudes to Employment* (2004) NOP.

14. Fletcher, W. (2002) *Beating the 24/7*, John Wiley & Sons.
15. *Investors in People Survey* (August 2004).
16. *The Economist* (p227 2004).
17. *Study of Marriage Patterns* (2004) The Cato Institute.
18. Goleman, D. (1996) *Emotional Intelligence*, Bloomsbury Publishing.

Chapter 3

1. *The Economist* (September 2004) Sir Alistair Morton's Obituary.
2. *A New Approach to the Valuation of Intangible Capital* (2004) National Bureau of Economic Research.
3. *Using the Performance Prism to Boost the Success of Mergers & Acquisitions* (2003) Accenture.
4. Myners, P. (2001) *The Myners Review of Institutional Investment in the UK*.
5. Kingsmill, D. (2003) *Accounting for People*, DTI.
6. Corporate Research Foundation (2005) *Britain's Top Employers*.
7. WPP Annual Report and Accounts (2003).
8. Higgs, Sir D. (2003) *Independent Review of the Role and Effectiveness of NEDs*, DTI.
9. Thomas, Sir Miles (1964) *Out on a Wing*, Michael Joseph.
10. *The Daily Telegraph* (May 2003).
11. The Sarbanes-Oxley Act (2002).
12. Accounting Standards Board (2003).
13. Vlasic, B. and Stretz, B. (2000) *Taken for a Ride: How Daimler-Benz Drove off with Chrysler*, John Wiley & Sons.
14. *Fifth Biennial TUC Survey Of Safety Representatives* (2004) TUC.

Chapter 4

1. 'The War for Talent' (1998), *The McKinsey Quarterly*, Issue 3.
2. Quoted in *Financial Times* (6 October 2004) 'Too many egos spoil the bank', p. 50.
3. Donkin, R. (2004) *HR and Reorganization: Managing the Challenge of Change*, CIPD.
4. *Gazette*, the Magazine of the John Lewis Partnership (2005), Vol. 87 (10).

Chapter 5

1. Milligan, A. and Smith, S. (2002) *Uncommon Practice: People Who Deliver A Great Brand Experience*, FT Prentice Hall, pp. 64–67.
2. Mercer (2003) *What's Working* (US/UK).
3. Financial Times/MORI survey (June 2003).
4. *Veracity Test* (February 2003) British Medical Association.
5. MORI (May, 2003) *Nestlé Family Monitor*.
6. See J.K. Galbraith's work on modern capitalism.

Chapter 6

1. *Unilever Code of Business Principles* (2003).
2. *The Concise Oxford Dictionary* (1964) Oxford University Press.
3. Herzberg, H. (1968) 'How do you Motivate Employees', *Harvard Business Review*, January–February, No. 6108.
4. Collins, J. and Porras, J. (1995) *Built to Last*, Century, Random House.
5. Martin, G. and Beaumont, P. (2003) *Branding and People Management*, CIPD.
6. Gratton, L. (2000) *Living Strategy: Putting People at the Heart of Corporate Purpose*, FT Prentice Hall.

Chapter 7

1. Survey Findings: *Emerging Trends in Internal Branding* (2000/2001), Lincolnshire, IL: Hewitt Associates LLC.
2. Dell and Ainspan (2001) *Engaging Employees Through Your Brand*, The Conference Board, Research Report 1288-01-RR.
3. *The Economist*, Employer Branding Survey (2003).
4. *Working Today: What Drives Employee Engagement* (2003) The Towers Perrin Talent Report.
5. *United States at Work 2000* (2000) AON Consulting.
6. *Linking Employee Satisfaction With Productivity, Performance and Satisfaction* (2003) Corporate Leadership Council.
7. *Are the 100 Best Better? An empirical investigation of the relationship between being a best employer and firm performance* (2000) Hewitt Associates.
8. *Maximizing Attendance, Managing Best Practice* (2000) The Industrial Society, No. 67.
9. *Achieving High Performance in Retail Banking, The Driving Role of Employee Opinion on Customer Satisfaction and Sales Performance* (2003) ISR.
10. *Engaging the American Worker* (2005) TNS North America Stakeholder Management Center.
11. *Understanding the People and Performance Link: Unlocking the Black Box* (2003) Work and Employment Research Centre, University of Bath, CIPD.
12. Heskett, J.L., Sasser, W.E. Jr and Schlesinger, L.A. (1997) *The Service Profit Chain: How Leading Companies Link Profit and Growth to Loyalty, Satisfaction and Value*, New York, Free Press.
13. *From People to Profits* (1999) The Institute for Employment Studies.
14. 'Q12 Workplace Survey', quoted from *Business Superbrands* (2000) published by Superbrands Ltd.
15. Kingsmill, D. (2003) *Accounting for People*, DTI.
16. *Linking Employee Satisfaction with Productivity, Performance and Customer Satisfaction* (2003) Corporate Leadership Council.

17. *Employee Commitment in Europe: Characteristics, Causes and Consequences* (2002) ISR.
18. *Work USA* (2002) Watson Wyatt Worldwide.
19. *A Portfolio of Best Companies to Work for in the UK* (2003) Frank Russell Company.
20. Gladwell, M. (2000) *The Tipping Point*, Little, Brown & Company.
21. 'Taking Tesco Global' (2002) *The McKinsey Quarterly*, No. 3.
22. Ulrich, D. (1997) *Human Resource Champions*, Harvard Business School Press.
23. Ambler, T. (2002) *Marketing and the Bottom Line*, FT Prentice Hall.
24. Pringle, H. and Gordon, W. (2001) *Brand Manners*, John Wiley & Sons.

Chapter 8

1. *Creating Competitive Advantage From your Employees: A Global Study Of Employee Engagement* (2004) ISR.
2. *Working Today: What Drives Employee Engagement* (2003) The Towers Perrin Talent Report.
3. *The Drivers of Employee Engagement* (2004) The Institute For Employment Studies.
4. *Work USA* (2002) Watson Wyatt.
5. *Employee Commitment Links to Bottom Line Success* (2002), TNS.
6. *UK plc: Leaders or Follower* (2001) ISR.
7. Hofstede, G. (1997) *Cultures and Organisations – Software of the Mind*, New York, McGraw-Hill.
8. Trompenaars, F. and Hampden-Turner, C. (1998) *Riding the Waves of Culture*, New York, McGraw-Hill.
9. Myers, I. and Briggs, M. (1995) *Gifts Differing, Understanding Personality Type*, Davies-Black.
10. 'The War for Talent' (1998) *The McKinsey Quarterly*, Issue 3.
11. Johnson, M. (2002) *Talent Magnet*, FT Prentice Hall.

Chapter 9

1. *The Sunday Times* (2004) 17 October, 'Finding Staff Who Fit Your Brand'.
2. Jones, R. (2000) *The Big Idea*, HarperCollins.
3. First Direct website.
4. *Building and Sustaining a High Performance Workforce* (2003) Horizon Watching Position Papers, www.naa.org/horizon
5. *The Times Top 100 Graduate Employers* (2004) High Fliers Publications.
6. Milligan, A and Smith, S. (2002) *Uncommon Practice: People Who Deliver a Great Brand Experience*, FT Prentice Hall.
7. Microsoft website.

Chapter 10

1. Ind, N. (2001) *Living The Brand: How To Transform Every Member of your Organisation into a Brand Champion*, Kogan Page.
2. Dyke, G. (2004) *Inside Story*, HarperCollins.

Chapter 11

1. *Employee Commitment in Europe: Characteristics, Causes and Consequences* (2002) ISR.
2. *The Ethical Employee* (2001) The Work Foundation.
3. *Good Companies, Better Employees* (2003) The Corporate Citizenship Company.
4. Vodafone website, www.vodafone.com
5. Unilever website, www.unilever.com
6. Johnson, M. (2004) *The New Rules of Engagement: Life–Work Balance and Employee Commitment*, CIPD.
7. *The Sunday Times* (2004) 17 October, 'Finding Staff Who Fit Your Brand'.
8. *The Drivers of Employee Engagement* (2004) The Institute for Employment Studies.
9. Michaels, E., Handfield-Jones, H. and Axelrod, B (2001) *The War for Talent*, Harvard Business School Press.
10. *Creating Competitive Advantage from your Employees: A Global Study of Employee Engagement* (2004) ISR.
11. Winter, J. and Jackson, C. (1999) *Riding the Wave, The New Global Career Culture*, Career Innovation Research Group.
12. *Engaging the American Worker* (2005) TNS North America Stakeholder Management Center.
13. *Vodafone Life* (May 2003) Issue 8.

Index

Index compiled by Annette Musker